GACE

Early Childhood Education Practice Questions

Mometrix

TEST PREPARATION

I0889224

DEAR FUTURE EXAM SUCCESS STORY

First of all, **THANK YOU** for purchasing Mometrix study materials!

Second, congratulations! You are one of the few determined test-takers who are committed to doing whatever it takes to excel on your exam. **You have come to the right place.** We developed these practice tests with one goal in mind: to deliver you the best possible approximation of the questions you will see on test day.

Standardized testing is one of the biggest obstacles on your road to success, which only increases the importance of doing well in the high-pressure, high-stakes environment of test day. Your results on this test could have a significant impact on your future, and these practice tests will give you the repetitions you need to build your familiarity and confidence with the test content and format to help you achieve your full potential on test day.

Your success is our success

We would love to hear from you! If you would like to share the story of your exam success or if you have any questions or comments in regard to our products, please contact us at **800-673-8175** or **support@mometrix.com**.

Thanks again for your business and we wish you continued success!

Sincerely,
The Mometrix Test Preparation Team

Written and edited by the Mometrix Exam Secrets Test Prep Team
Printed in the United States of America

TABLE OF CONTENTS

Practice Test #1

1. Which of the following statements is accurate according to research regarding students who are revising and rewriting?

a. Students only correct their mechanical errors in revisions.
b. Students often incorporate new ideas when they rewrite.
c. Students retain their original writing goals during revision.
d. Students' planning in prewriting is unaffected in rewriting.

2. With a teacher's guidance, a class brainstorms main ideas, topics, or concepts from a text. Students choose a select number of these ideas and copy them onto separate index cards. The students then individually review the text, recording any supporting evidence on the notecard with the applicable main idea. This activity would be an excellent pre-lesson for teaching which skill set?

a. Working as a group to interpret a text and write an appropriate and realistic sequel, focusing on interpretive comprehension and creative writing
b. Silent reading as a form of comprehension practice
c. Organizing ideas for writing a cohesive and persuasive essay or research paper that asserts supported arguments with valid supporting evidence
d. Literal and figurative comprehension, as well as contributing to group discussions via oral communication skills

3. A teacher is working with a group of third graders at the same reading level. Her goal is to improve reading fluency. She asks each child in turn to read a page from a book about mammal young. She asks the children to read with expression. She also reminds them they don't need to stop between each word; they should read as quickly as they comfortably can. She cautions them, however, not to read so quickly that they leave out or misread a word. The teacher knows the components of reading fluency are:

a. Speed, drama, and comprehension
b. Cohesion, rate, and prosody
c. Understanding, rate, and prosody
d. Rate, accuracy, and prosody

4. *Carat, carrot, to, two,* and *too* share something in common. They are:

a. Nouns
b. Monosyllabic
c. Homophones
d. Diphthongs

5. Which of the following statements adheres to Information Literacy Standards?

a. Students accessing information must critically evaluate it and its sources before using it.
b. Students accessing information should acquire as much information as possible about their topic.
c. Students accessing information efficiently sacrifice incidental learning.
d. Students accessing information must avoid using it for purposes it was not meant to serve.

6. Third-grade students typically receive their spelling word lists each Monday so that they can practice them at home before the test on Friday. While their teacher is pleased that the students usually receive high grades on spelling tests, she observes that they misspell those same words when writing in journals or doing classwork. How should this teacher modify her instruction?

a. Post a list of vocabulary words when the students are writing to help them recall correct spellings.
b. Integrate spelling words into writing, reading, grammar, phonics, and other activities to help students learn the words in a variety of contexts.
c. Provide more time, such as a two-week period, between tests so that students have more time to study.
d. Review the words before certain activities to increase immediate recall of correct spellings.

7. Of the three tiers of words, the most important words for direct instruction are:

a. Tier-one words
b. Common words
c. Tier-two words
d. Words with Latin roots

8. Which student is most likely to need referral to a reading specialist for assessment, special instruction, or intervention?

a. Annabel: a second-grade student who tends to skip over words or phrases when she reads, affecting her comprehension of the text.
b. Cliff: a kindergarten student who is already reading simple chapter books with his parents at home or in class.
c. Noelle: a first grader who avoids any activity in which she must read, both aloud or silently, preferring to ask an adult to read the text for her first.
d. Barrett: a third grader who often confuses the sounds of certain letters, such as /b/ and /d/ or /v/ and /u/.

9. According to the MLA guidelines for in-text citations in research papers, when can the citation include one author's name and *et al* for any other authors of a single source?

a. When there is more than one author
b. When there are two or three authors
c. When there are three or more authors
d. When there are four or more authors

10. A child in kindergarten is most likely to be referred to a speech-language pathologist if the child does not correctly produce which of the following phonemes?

a. /p/ as in pepper or poppies
b. /ʒ/ as in mirage or measure
c. /v/ as in velvet, valve, or value
d. /s/ as in see, yes, or asking

11. Which of the following best explains the importance prior knowledge brings to the act of reading?

a. Prior knowledge is information the student gets through researching a topic prior to reading the text. A student who is well-prepared through such research is better able to decode a text and retain its meaning.
b. Prior knowledge is knowledge the student brings from previous life or learning experiences to the act of reading. It is not possible for a student to fully comprehend new knowledge without first integrating it with prior knowledge.
c. Prior knowledge is predictive. It motivates the student to look for contextual clues in the reading and predict what is likely to happen next.
d. Prior knowledge is not important to any degree to the act of reading, because every text is self-contained and therefore seamless. Prior knowledge is irrelevant in this application.

12. A fourth-grade teacher had her students write haiku in order to promote the students' _________.

a. reading comprehension
b. vocabulary
c. word identification skills
d. confidence

13. What is a mnemonic device?

a. A saying or image used to help remember a complex concept
b. A tool that increases physical relaxation during a test
c. An old-fashioned torture device involving repeated testing
d. A tool for selecting answers on tests

14. Of the following, which statement is true about instruction in the alphabetic principle?

a. Letter-sound relationships with the highest utility should be the earliest ones introduced.
b. The instruction of letter-sound correspondences should always be done in word context.
c. Letter-sound relationship practice times should only be assigned apart from other lessons.
d. Letter-sound relationship practice should focus on new relationships, not go over old ones.

15. Early in the school year, all members of a group of kindergarten students are able to chant the alphabet. The teacher is now teaching the students what the alphabet looks like in written form. The teacher points to a letter, and the students vocalize the corresponding sound. Alternatively, the teacher vocalizes a phoneme and a student points to it on the alphabet chart. The teacher is using _____________ in her instruction.

a. letter–sound correspondence
b. rote memorization
c. predictive analysis
d. segmentation

16. Components of explicit instruction include:

a. Clarifying the goal, modeling strategies, and offering explanations geared to a student's level of understanding
b. Determining the goal, offering strategies, and asking questions designed to ascertain whether understanding has been reached
c. Reassessing the goal, developing strategies, and determining whether further reassessing of the goal is required
d. Objectifying the goal, assessing strategies, and offering explanations geared toward a student's level of understanding

17. Which choice most appropriately fills the blanks in this statement? "In writing, ________ is the overall choice of language in a piece of writing; ________ is a specialized terminology, used in a discipline, that is not readily understood by readers outside of that discipline."

a. jargon, style
b. vocabulary, diction
c. diction, jargon
d. style, vocabulary

18. Regarding these elements of print awareness in literacy development, which is true?

a. All students with normal development can differentiate printed words from spaces.
b. To identify initial and final letters in words, students must identify words vs. spaces.
c. The only students not automatically knowing left-right directionality are certain ELLs.
d. Being able to identify basic punctuation is not important to reading comprehension.

19. It is the beginning of the school year. To determine which second-grade students might need support, the reading teacher wants to identify those who are reading below grade level. She works with students one at a time. She gives each child a book at a second-grade reading level and asks the child to read out loud for two minutes. Which students will need reading support?

a. Only students who read fewer than 100 words in the time given
b. All students who read fewer than 200 words in the time given
c. All students who read more than 100 words in the time given
d. Only students who read more than 200 words in the time given

20. When working with English language learners, the teacher should:

a. Avoid idioms and slang, involve students in hands-on activities, reference students' prior knowledge, and speak slowly.
b. Speak slowly, use monosyllabic words whenever possible, repeat each sentence three times before moving to the next sentence, and employ idioms but not slang.
c. Use monosyllabic words whenever possible, repeat key instructions three times but not in a row, reference students' prior knowledge, and have students keep a journal of new vocabulary.
d. Have students keep a journal of new vocabulary, reference students' prior knowledge, speak slowly, and involve students in hands-on activities.

21. Which of the following processes used in writing is the most complex?

a. Evaluation
b. Application
c. Comprehension
d. Knowledge recall

22. When a teacher instructs elementary school students in analyzing phonetically-regular words, which of the following would best represent a sequence from simpler to progressively more complex?

a. Long vowels, short vowels, consonant blends, CVC (consonant-vowel-consonant) and other common patterns, individual phonemes, blending phonemes, types of syllables, onsets and rimes
b. Onsets and rimes, short vowels, consonant blends, long vowels, blending phonemes, CVC and other common patterns, types of syllables, individual phonemes
c. Types of syllables, onsets and rimes, CVC and other common patterns, consonant blends, blending phonemes, individual phonemes, long vowels, short vowels
d. Individual phonemes, blending phonemes, onsets and rimes, short vowels, long vowels, consonant blends, CVC and other common patterns, types of syllables

23. Which text(s) are likely to foster the greatest enthusiasm for reading and literature among students?

a. Free choice of reading texts, provided that students complete class assignments, projects, and discussions
b. An all-in-one textbook that includes all reading material for the year, study guides, and sample test questions
c. A variety of texts, including books, magazines, newspapers, stories from oral traditions, poetry, music, and films
d. A small selection of current best-selling books for children, some of which the children may already have read and liked

24. Coarticulation affects:

a. Blending awareness
b. Phonemic awareness
c. Sequencing
d. Aural awareness

25. Some of the students in Mr. Smith's fourth-grade class cannot decode words well enough to read fluently in class. He knows they are well behind grade level and that he needs to provide them with activities that will allow them to be successful, building skills and confidence at the same time. Which activity would be best for this purpose?

a. Enlist the parents' help by sending home a weekly list of sight words that the students can practice and memorize, decreasing the need to decode when they read.
b. Show the students how to create words out of movable alphabet tiles or magnetic letters, building (encoding) words as they sound them out.
c. Provide the children with early childhood readers that contain only very simple words so that the children will not feel badly as they read.
d. Allow those children having trouble to stop each time they reach a challenging word and sound it out carefully, recording it to a list that will be studied for homework.

26. Which of the following involves evaluative reading comprehension?

a. Identifying an author's point of view
b. Explaining the author's point of view
c. Identifying the main idea of the text
d. Predicting what will happen in a text

27. *Since, therefore,* and *accordingly* are examples of which type of signal words?

a. Common, or basic, signal words
b. Compare/contrast words
c. Cause–effect words
d. Temporal sequencing words

28. Which of the following linguistic domains relates primarily to the meanings of words?

a. Graphophonic
b. Semantic
c. Syntactic
d. Pragmatic

29. Which adult would be most effective in helping a student who frequently mispronounces sounds both in reading and in conversation?

a. A whole language specialist
b. A speech pathologist
c. A paraprofessional
d. A psychologist

30. Of the following, which represents an indirect way in which students receive instruction in and learn vocabulary?

a. Being exposed repeatedly to vocabulary in multiple teaching contexts
b. Being exposed to vocabulary when adults read aloud to them
c. Being pre-taught specific words found in text prior to reading
d. Being taught vocabulary words over extended periods of time

31. A teacher is teaching students using rime analogies to support reading comprehension. Which of the following skills best relates to the use of rime analogies?

a. Students will be able to identify and use metaphors and similes.
b. Students will be able to identify and use similar sounding words.
c. Students will be able to identify and use similarly spelled words.
d. Students will be able to identify and use figures of speech.

32. Scholars have identified three major categories of connections that students make when reading: text-to-self connections, text-to-world connections, and text-to-text connections. Which of the following student statements is an example of a connection of text to the world?

a. These mythic gods have more power but feel and act like humans.
b. This novel is set during a period I learned about in my history textbook.
c. I can relate to how the main character felt about being controlled.
d. The protagonist reminds me of the main character in another story.

33. Learning to construct a reading response would be most beneficial in enhancing which language skill?

a. Oral presentation
b. Comprehension
c. Fluency
d. Learning a second language

34. Which of the following ways of presenting information is best for showing change over time?

a. Tables
b. Maps
c. Graphs
d. Charts

35. A teacher is working with a student who is struggling with reading. The teacher gives him a story with key words missing:

> The boy wanted to take the dog for a walk. The boy opened the door. The _____ ran out. The ___ looked for the dog. When he found the dog, he was very ______.

The student is able to fill in the blanks by considering:

a. Syntax. Oftentimes, word order gives enough clues that a reader can predict what happens next.
b. Pretext. By previewing the story, the student can deduce the missing words.
c. Context. By considering the other words in the story, the student can determine the missing words.
d. Sequencing. By putting the ideas in logical order, the student can determine the missing words.

36. Which statement is most accurate about social contexts of L1 and L2 acquisition?

a. L2 learning can occur equally in varied contexts, from natural to educational, but L1 learning cannot.
b. L1s are only learned in natural contexts, while L2s are learned in educational contexts.
c. Variations in L2 proficiency can result from the different contexts of the learning of L2s.
d. L2s are never learned in natural contexts, as they are not the learners' natural languages.

37. Which of the following choices would be the best comprehensive project for a fourth-grade class at the end of the school year?

a. The students take an open-book, cumulative test that measures the students' understanding of various concepts and genres through multiple choice, short-answer, and short-essay questions.
b. Assign children to a group in which they will read and adapt a short play. Each group will perform its play with costumes and staging while the rest of the class will serve as audience members. Audience members will write short responses to what they have seen, which will be shared with the performers.
c. Each student picks a topic about which they would like to conduct independent research. The students will read a variety of texts from different sources to learn more about the topic and then use that information to create a presentation for the class. The use of technology and media is encouraged in presentations.
d. The students take a field trip to the local university to visit the English Department. The students are permitted to sit in on a class lecture and speak to professors about the program. Students also get a chance to interact with college students and find out what literacy skills are most important for a successful college experience.

38. How should teachers best instruct students in writing?

a. In connection with reading only
b. By itself to focus student attention
c. With relation to reading and speaking
d. Related to listening, reading, and speaking

39. A teacher has a child who does not volunteer in class. When the teacher asks the student a question the student can answer, she does so with as few words as possible. The teacher isn't sure how to best help the child. She should:

a. Leave the child alone. She is clearly very shy and will be embarrassed by having attention drawn to her. She is learning in her own way.
b. Ask two or three highly social children to include this girl in their activities. She is shy, and she probably won't approach them on her own.
c. Observe the child over the course of a week or two. Draw her into conversation and determine if her vocabulary is limited, if she displays emotional problems, or if her reticence could have another cause. Note how the child interacts with others in the class. Does she ever initiate conversation? If another child initiates, does she respond?
d. Refer her to the school counselor immediately. It is clear the child is suffering from either a low IQ or serious problems at home.

40. Which of the following is the source of the silent *b* in the English word *debt*?

a. A Middle English root word
b. An Old English root word
c. A Latin root word
d. A Greek root word

41. Which choice describes the most complete method of displaying student achievement or progress in language arts?

a. A written report or story that demonstrates a student's knowledge of grammar, spelling, comprehension, and writing skills.
b. Either a norm- or criterion-referenced test that breaks language skills into small subsets and provides achievement levels for each skill.
c. A portfolio containing a log of stories or books the student has read, rates of reading fluency, writing samples, creative projects, and spelling, grammar, and comprehension tests/quizzes.
d. A year-end project in which the student presents what he or she has learned from a student-chosen book; the student must read an excerpt of the story and display a visual aid highlighting important information from the story or literary techniques used by the author.

42. Among four categories of media that teachers instruct students to identify, in which one are books primarily classified?

a. Media used in one-on-one communication
b. Media used for entertainment
c. Media to inform many people
d. Media for persuading people

43. A student is able to decode most words fluently and has a borderline/acceptable vocabulary, but his reading comprehension is quite low. He can be helped with instructional focus on:

a. Strategies to increase comprehension and to build vocabulary
b. Strategies to increase comprehension and to be able to identify correct syntactical usage
c. Strategies to improve his understanding of both content and context
d. Strategies to build vocabulary and to improve his understanding of both content and context

44. The following sentence is which of the following sentence types?

The questions in this test can give you an idea of what kinds of questions you might find on the actual test; however, they are not duplicates of the actual test questions, which cover the same subject material but may differ in form and content.

a. Simple
b. Complex
c. Compound
d. Compound-complex

45. Which assessment will determine a student's ability to identify initial, medial, blended, final, segmented, and manipulated "units"?

a. Phonological awareness assessment
b. High-frequency word assessment
c. Reading fluency assessment
d. Comprehension quick-check

46. A student identifies a text to read independently. According to an informal reading inventory the teacher just conducted, the student understands 48 percent of words in isolation that this text includes, reads words contained in this text with 90 percent accuracy in context, and correctly answers 68 percent of comprehension questions at this text's reading level. What does this indicate to the teacher?

a. This text is at the student's independent level; the teacher approves the student's selection.
b. This text is at the student's frustration level; the teacher helps the student find another text.
c. This text is at the student's instructional level, and the teacher approves it for guided reading.
d. This text is at some reading level that cannot be identified only from the student information.

47. Which of the following choices represents the smallest unit of language that possesses semantic meaning?

a. Morpheme
b. Grapheme
c. Phoneme
d. Word stem

48. Which of the following expressions is equivalent to $-3x(x-2)^2$?

a. $-3x^3 + 6x^2 - 12x$
b. $-3x^3 - 12x^2 + 12x$
c. $-3x^2 + 6x$
d. $-3x^3 + 12x^2 - 12x$

49. McKenzie shades $\frac{1}{5}$ of a piece of paper. Then, she shades an additional area $\frac{1}{5}$ the size of what she just shaded. Next, she shades another area $\frac{1}{5}$ as large as the previous one. As she continues the process to infinity, what is the limit of the shaded fraction of the paper?

a. $\frac{1}{5}$
b. $\frac{1}{4}$
c. $\frac{1}{3}$
d. $\frac{1}{2}$

50. Which of the following represents the net of a triangular prism?

a. 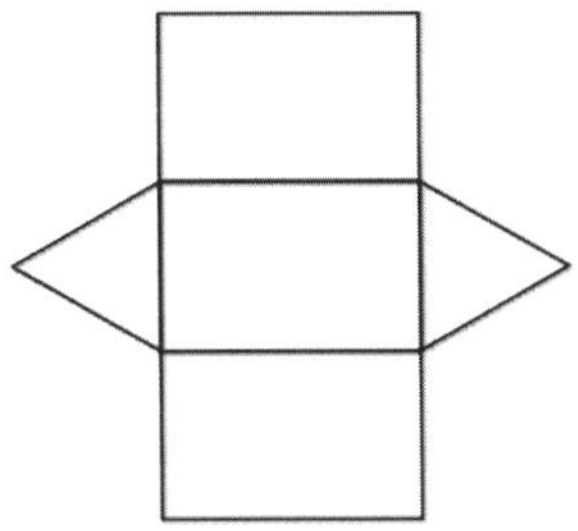

b. 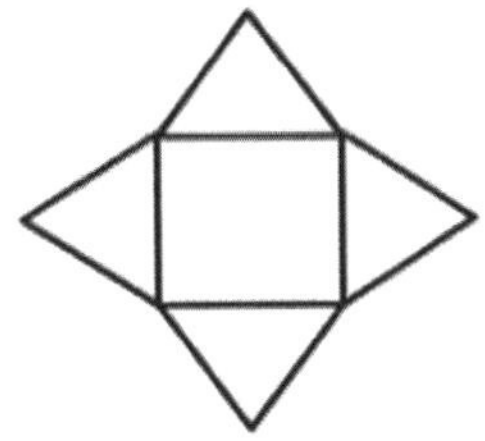

c. 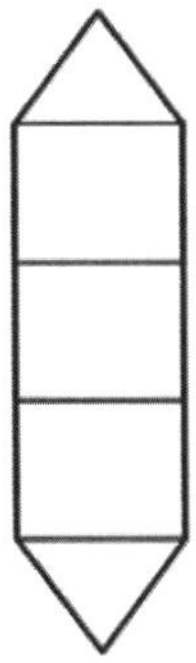

d. 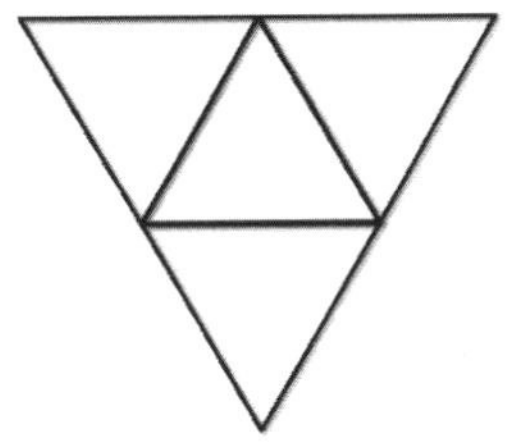

51. Andrew rolls a die. What is the probability he gets a 4 or an even number?

a. $\frac{1}{4}$
b. $\frac{1}{2}$
c. $\frac{2}{3}$
d. $\frac{3}{4}$

52. Which of the following learning goals is most appropriate for a second-grade unit on personal financial literacy?

a. The students will be able to calculate how money saved can accumulate into a larger amount over time.
b. The students will be able to balance a simple budget.
c. The students will be able to identify the costs and benefits of planned and unplanned spending decisions.
d. The students will be able to define money earned as income.

53. What is the value of the expression $-3 \times 5^2 + 2(4 - 18) + 33$?

a. −130
b. −70
c. −20
d. 74

54. Claus has \$20 to spend at the local fair. The entrance fee is \$2. 50, and tickets for the booths are \$2 each. Which of the following inequalities represents the number of tickets x that Claus can afford with his \$20?

a. $2.50x + 2x \leq 20$
b. $2.50 + 2x \leq 20$
c. $2x \leq 20 + 2.50$
d. $2.50 + 2x \geq 20x$

55. A teacher is assessing the students' understanding of the appropriate units for length, area, and volume. Which of the following only lists units of area?

a. in^2, mm^2, ft^2
b. yd, yd^2, yd^3
c. mm, cm, m
d. m^2, s^2, km^2

56. Ms. Elliott asks her fifth-grade students, "Do you prefer chocolate or vanilla ice cream?" If the probability of her students preferring chocolate ice cream is 0.6, what is the probability of her students preferring vanilla ice cream?

a. 0.6
b. 0.4
c. 0.3
d. 0.5

57. While teaching the concept of addition, a first-grade teacher gives each student two dice to use as manipulatives. Which of the following types of representation is this teacher using to communicate this concept?

a. Concrete
b. Verbal
c. Graphic
d. Pictorial

58. The variables x and y have a linear relationship. The table below shows a few sample values. Which of the following graphs correctly represents the linear equation relating x and y?

x	y
−2	−11
−1	-8
0	-5
1	-2
2	1

a. 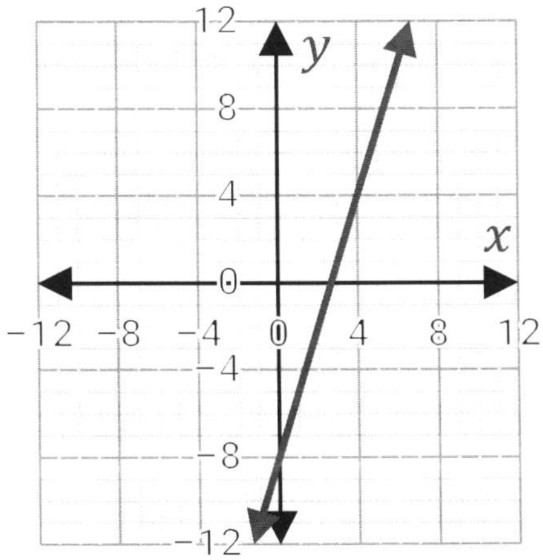

b. 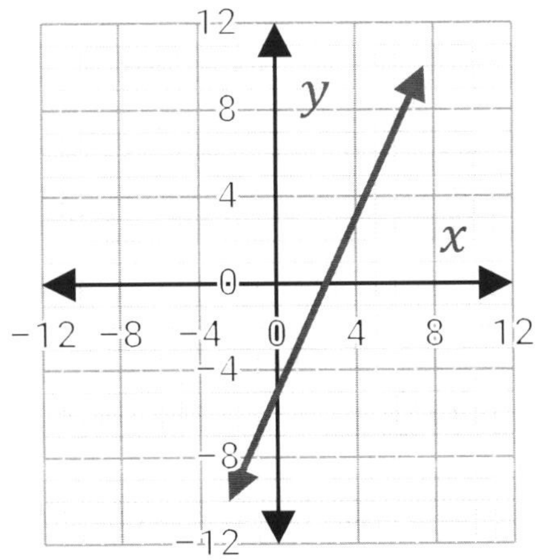

c. 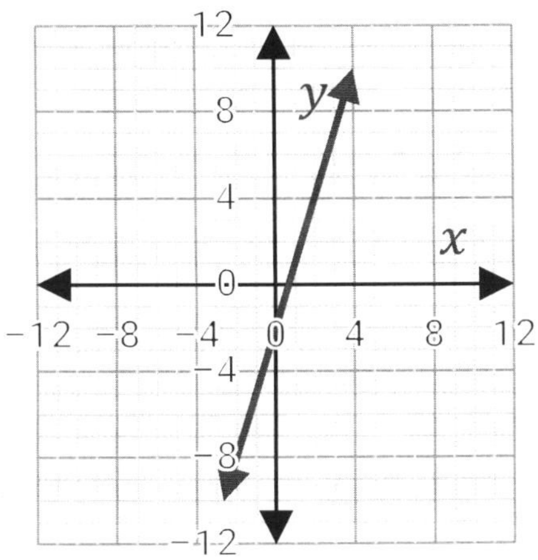

d. 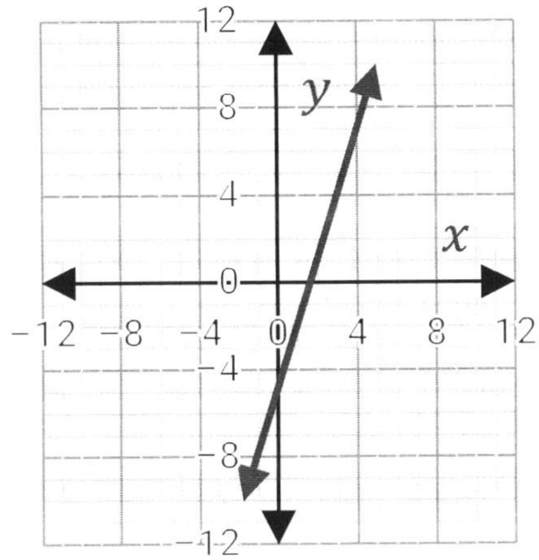

59. What is the midpoint of the line segment below?

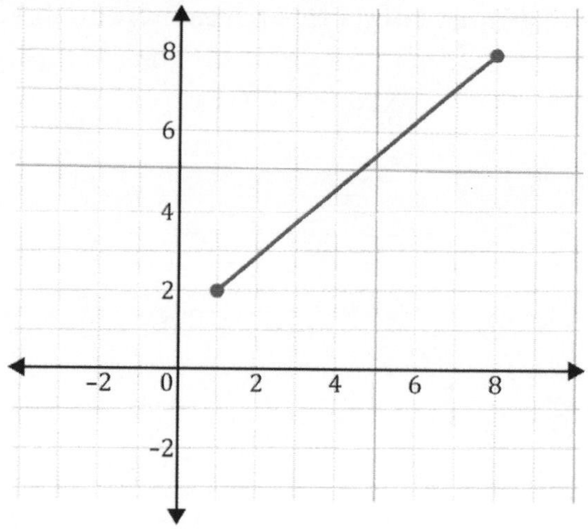

a. (3.5,4)
b. (4,4)
c. (4.5,5)
d. (5,5)

60. Ann must walk from Point A to Point B and then to Point C. Finally, she will walk back to Point A. If each unit represents 5 miles, which of the following BEST represents the total distance she will have walked?

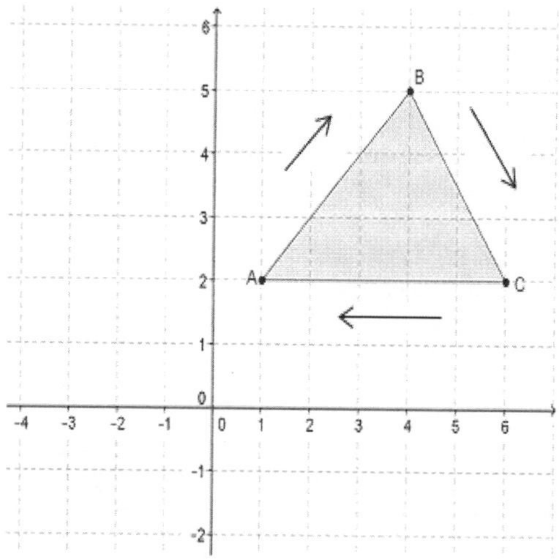

a. 42 miles
b. 48 miles
c. 56 miles
d. 64 miles

61. When planning a unit on linear equations, a teacher would most likely include discussion on which of the following topics?

a. Conjugating to remove irrational denominators
b. Slope of a straight line
c. Order of operations
d. Characteristics of the diagonals of various quadrilaterals

62. Two companies offer monthly cell phone plans, both of which include free text messaging. Company A charges a $25 monthly fee plus five cents per minute of phone conversation, while Company B charges a $50 monthly fee and offers unlimited calling. At what total duration of monthly calls do both companies charge the same amount?

a. 500 hours
b. 8 hours and 33 minutes
c. 8 hours and 20 minutes
d. 5 hours

63. Solve the system of equations.

$$3x + 4y = 2$$
$$2x + 6y = -2$$

a. $\left(0, \frac{1}{2}\right)$
b. $\left(\frac{2}{5}, \frac{1}{5}\right)$
c. $(2, -1)$
d. $\left(-1, \frac{5}{4}\right)$

64. Identify the cross-section polygon formed by a plane containing the given points on the cube.

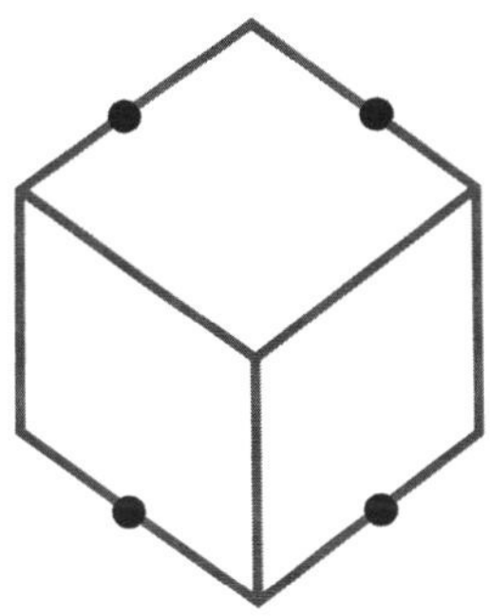

a. Rectangle
b. Trapezoid
c. Pentagon
d. Hexagon

65. In order to analyze the real estate market for two different zip codes within the city, a realtor examined the most recent 100 home sales in each zip code. She considered a house which sold within the first month of its listing to have a market time of one month; likewise, she considered a house to have a market time of two months if it sold after having been on the market for more than one month but before the end of the second month. Using this definition of market time, she determined the frequency of sales by the number of months on the market. The results are displayed below. Which of the following is a true statement for these data?

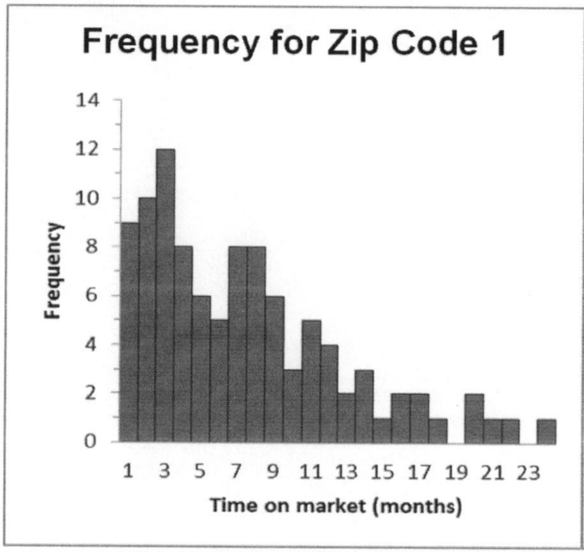

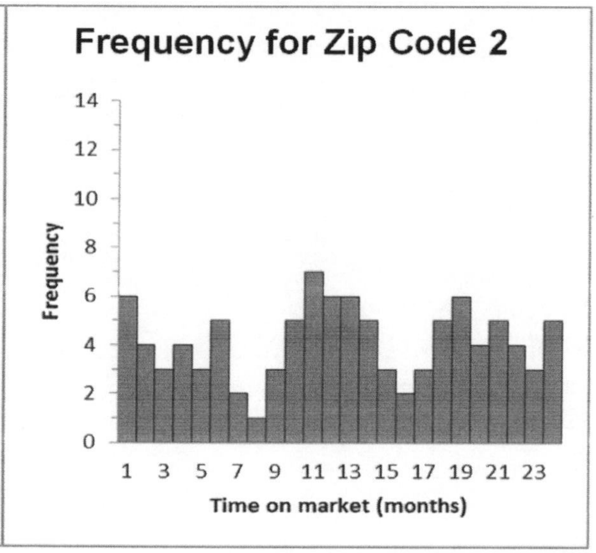

a. The median time a house spent on the market in Zip Code 1 is five months less than Zip Code 2.
b. On average, a house spent seven months longer on the market in Zip Code 2 than in Zip Code 1.
c. The mode time on the market is higher for Zip Code 1 than for Zip Code 2.
d. The median time on the market is less than the mean time on the market for Zip Code 1.

66. Jason decides to donate 1% of his annual salary to a local charity. If his annual salary is $45,000, how much will he donate?

a. $4.50
b. $45
c. $450
d. $4,500

67. Kevin saves $3 during Month 1. During each subsequent month, he plans to save 4 more dollars than he saved during the previous month. Which of the following equations represents the amount he will save during the nth month?

a. $a_n = 3n - 1$
b. $a_n = 3n + 4$
c. $a_n = 4n + 3$
d. $a_n = 4n - 1$

68. A tree with a height of 15 feet casts a shadow that is 5 feet in length. A man standing at the base of the shadow formed by the tree is 6 feet tall. How long is the shadow cast by the man?

a. 1.5 feet
b. 2 feet
c. 2.5 feet
d. 3 feet

69. A coin is tossed 300 times. How many of those tosses can you expect to show heads?

a. 50
b. 100
c. 150
d. 200

70. Mr. Mancelli teaches fifth-grade math. He is making prize bags for the winners of a math game. If he has eight candy bars and twelve packages of gum, what is the largest number of identical prize bags he can make without having any left-over candy bars or packages of gum?

a. 2
b. 4
c. 6
d. 8

71. Which of the following goals is appropriate in the category of algebraic reasoning for first-grade students?

a. Students represent one- and two-step problems involving addition and subtraction of whole numbers to 1,000 using pictorial models, number lines, and equations.
b. Students represent real-world relationships using number pairs in a table and verbal descriptions.
c. Students represent word problems involving addition and subtraction of whole numbers up to 20 using concrete and pictorial models and number sentences.
d. Students recite numbers up to at least 100 by ones and tens beginning with any given number.

72. Which of the following descriptions best fits a hexagonal prism?

a. 8 faces, 18 edges, 12 vertices
b. 6 faces, 18 edges, 12 vertices
c. 8 faces, 16 edges, 8 vertices
d. 6 faces, 14 edges, 10 vertices

73. Addison tosses a six-sided die twelve times and records the results in the table below.

Toss	1	2	3	4	5	6	7	8	9	10	11	12
Results	2	5	1	2	3	6	6	2	4	5	4	3

Which of the following statements is true?

a. The experimental probability of tossing a 6 is greater than the theoretical probability.
b. The experimental probability of tossing a 3 is greater than the theoretical probability.
c. The experimental probability of tossing a 1 is greater than the theoretical probability.
d. The experimental probability of tossing a 2 is greater than the theoretical probability.

74. If $f(x) = \frac{x^3-2x+1}{3x}$, what is $f(2)$?

a. $\frac{1}{3}$
b. $\frac{1}{2}$
c. $\frac{5}{6}$
d. $\frac{5}{2}$

75. What is the distance on a coordinate plane from $(-8, 6)$ to $(4, 3)$?

a. $\sqrt{139}$
b. $\sqrt{147}$
c. $\sqrt{153}$
d. $\sqrt{161}$

76. $A = \{9, 4, -3, 8, 6, 0\}$ and $B = \{-4, 2, 8, 9, 0\}$. What is $A \cup B$?

a. $\{9,8,0\}$
b. $\{9,4,-3,8,6,0,-4,2\}$
c. $\emptyset$
d. $\{9,8,0,2,4\}$

77. On a floor plan drawn at a scale of $1 : 100$, the area of a rectangular room is 30 cm^2. What is the actual area of the room?

a. 30,000 cm^2
b. 300 m^2
c. 3,000 m^2
d. 30 m^2

78. A developer decides to build a fence around a neighborhood park, which is positioned on a rectangular lot. Rather than fencing along the lot line, he fences x feet from each of the lot's boundaries. By fencing a rectangular space 141 yd^2 smaller than the lot, the developer saves \$432 in fencing materials, which cost \$12 per linear foot. How much does he spend?

a. \$160
b. \$456
c. \$3,168
d. The answer cannot be determined from the given information.

Refer to the following for question 79:

The box-and-whisker plot displays student test scores by class period.

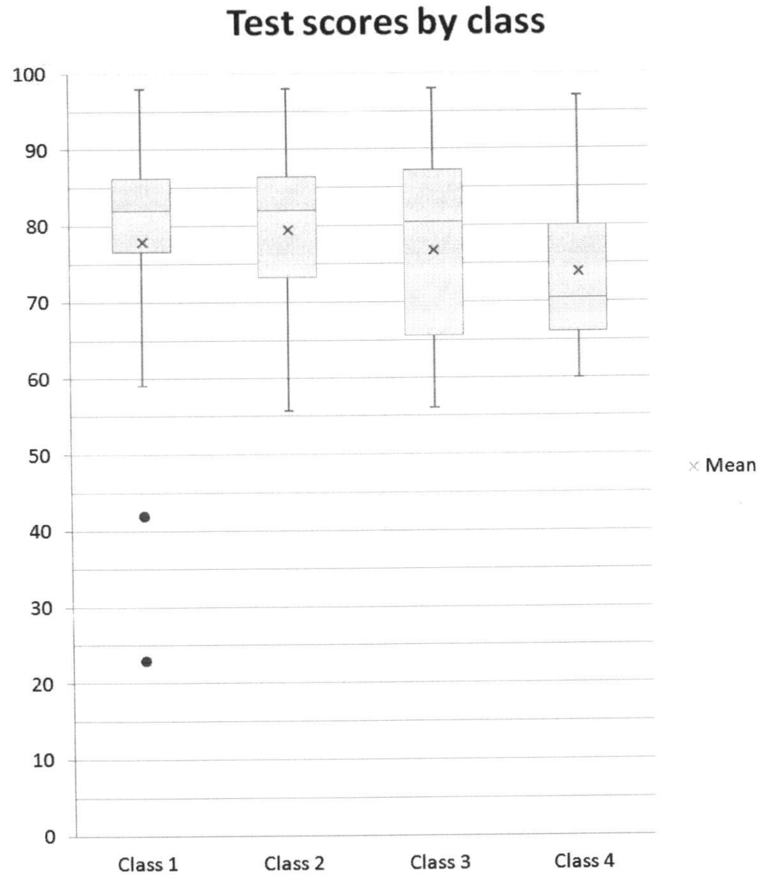

79. Which of the following statements is true of the data?

a. The mean better reflects student performance in class 1 than the median.
b. The mean test score for class 1 and 2 is the same.
c. The median test score for class 1 and 2 is the same.
d. The median test score is above the mean for class 4.

80. A circular bracelet contains 5 charms, A, B, C, D, and E, attached at specific points around the bracelet, with the clasp located between charms A and B. The bracelet is unclasped and stretched out into a straight line. On the resulting linear bracelet, charm C is between charms A and B, charm D is between charms A and C, and charm E is between charms C and D. Which of these statements is (are) necessarily true?

I. The distance between charms B and E is greater than the distance between charms A and D.
II. Charm E is between charms B and D.
III. The distance between charms D and E is less than the distance of bracelet between charms A and C.

a. I, II, and III
b. II and III
c. II only
d. None of these must be true.

81. A gift box has a length of 14 inches, a height of 8 inches, and a width of 6 inches. How many square inches of wrapping paper are needed to wrap the box?

a. 56
b. 244
c. 488
d. 672

82. Eli rolls a six-sided die and tosses a coin. What is the probability that he gets a prime number or tails?

a. $\frac{1}{4}$
b. $\frac{1}{3}$
c. $\frac{1}{2}$
d. $\frac{3}{4}$

83. Ms. Chen is instructing her students on divisibility rules. Which of the following rules can be used to determine if a number is divisible by 6?

a. The last digit of the number is divisible by 2 or 3.
b. The number ends in 6.
c. The number is divisible by 2 and 3.
d. The last two digits of the number are divisible by 6.

84. Marcus is mowing yards and doing odd jobs to earn money for a new video game system that costs $325. Marcus only charges $6.50 per hour. Which of the following equations represents the number of hours Marcus needs to work to earn $325?

a. $6.50x = 325$
b. $6.50 + x = 325$
c. $325x = 6.50$
d. $6.50x + 325 = x$

85. Which of the following BEST describes the significance of the US Supreme Court's decision in the Dred Scott case?

a. The ruling effectively declared slavery to be a violation of the Constitution.
b. The ruling guaranteed full citizenship rights to freed slaves.
c. The ruling turned many Southerners against the Supreme Court.
d. The ruling furthered the gap between North and South and hastened the Civil War.

86. Which of the following is true regarding the Tropic of Capricorn?

a. It separates the northern and southern hemispheres.
b. It separates the eastern and western hemispheres.
c. It is the southernmost latitude at which the sun can appear directly overhead at noon.
d. It is the northernmost latitude at which the sun can appear directly overhead at noon.

87. The Seven Years' War, called the French and Indian War by the Colonists:

a. Was the precursor to the American Revolution
b. Was a conflict related to European colonization
c. Primarily took place in Canada
d. Ended European conquests

88. Which of the following statements is NOT an accurate statement about the Puritans in England?

a. The Puritans unconditionally gave all their support to the English Reformation.
b. The Puritans saw the Church of England as too much like the Catholic Church.
c. The Puritans became a chief political power because of the English Civil War.
d. The Puritans' clergy mainly departed from the Church of England after 1662.

89. Which part of a hurricane features the strongest winds and greatest rainfall?

a. Eye wall
b. Front
c. Eye
d. Outward spiral

90. Most federal judges have served as local judges, lawyers, and law professors. These are ________ qualifications.

a. Formal
b. Required
c. Informal
d. Recommended

91. Of the following, who was NOT a dispatch rider notifying Americans of British troop movements reported by American surveillance in 1775?

a. Paul Revere
b. William Dawes
c. John Parker
d. Samuel Prescott

92. The physical geography of a region most directly affects which of the following?

a. The religious beliefs of the native population
b. The family structure of the native population
c. The dietary preferences of the native population
d. The language spoken by the native population

93. The price of oil drops dramatically, saving soda pop manufacturers great amounts of money spent on making soda pop and delivering their product to market. Prices for soda pop, however, stay the same. This is an example of what?

a. Sticky prices
b. Indiscriminate costs
c. Stable demand
d. Aggregate expenditure

94. What does the 10th Amendment establish?

a. Any power not given to the federal government belongs to the states or the people.
b. The president is responsible for executing and enforcing laws created by Congress.
c. Congress has the authority to declare war.
d. The Supreme Court has the authority to interpret the Constitution.

95. What did the Mason-Dixon Line divide?

a. The East from the West before the western states were incorporated
b. The East from the West along the Mississippi River
c. The North from the South before the Civil War
d. The Senate from the House of Representatives

96. The philosophy of the late 17th-18th centuries that influenced the Constitution was from the Age of:

a. Enlightenment
b. Empire
c. Discovery
d. Industry

97. Which geographic features were most conducive to the development of early civilizations?

a. Rivers
b. Deserts
c. Forests
d. Mountains

98. What portion of the federal budget is dedicated to transportation, education, national resources, the environment, and international affairs?

a. Mandatory spending
b. Discretionary spending
c. Undistributed offsetting receipts
d. Official budget outlays

99. Thomas Jefferson embraced a theological philosophy called deism, which promotes which of the following?

a. Abolition
b. Atheism
c. Separation of church and state
d. A theocratic central government

100. When the Senate held an impeachment hearing against Andrew Johnson for overstepping his authority, what did they invoke?

a. Checks and balances
b. Bicameralism
c. Legislative oversight
d. Supremacy

101. What are the first ten amendments to the Constitution more commonly known as?

a. The Civil Rights Act
b. Common law
c. The Equal Protection clause
d. The Bill of Rights

102. A country's currency increases in value on foreign currency exchange markets. What will happen as a result?

I. Exports will drop
II. Imports will rise
III. The balance of payments will rise

a. I only
b. II only
c. I and II
d. II and III

103. Which statement about factors related to the growth of the US economy between 1945 and 1970 is NOT correct?

a. The Baby Boom's greatly increased birth rates contributed to economic growth during this time.
b. The reduction in military spending after World War II contributed to the stronger US economy.
c. Government programs and growing affluence nearly quadrupled college enrollments in 20 years.
d. Increased mobility and bigger families caused fast suburban expansion, especially in the Sunbelt.

104. The civil rights act that outlawed segregation in schools and public places also did which of the following?

a. Gave minorities the right to vote
b. Established women's right to vote
c. Outlawed unequal voter registration
d. Provided protection for children

105. Which of the following world religions is the oldest?

a. Greek Stoicism
b. Confucianism
c. Christianity
d. Judaism

106. Which of the following is associated with market failure?

I. When a firm in a non-competitive industry hires labor at a lower wage
II. When the firms in a non-competitive industry create less than the efficient amount of a good or service
III. When production of a good creates negative externalities born by third parties
IV. Public goods

a. I and II only
b. I and III only
c. I, II, and III only
d. I, II, III, and IV

107. Which of the following statements is NOT correct regarding these religions under the Roman Empire?

a. The Romans generally protected the Jews until the rebellion in Judea (66 AD).
b. Julius Caesar circumvented Roman law to help Jews have freedom of worship.
c. The Druids were a religious group that the Romans ignored but also tolerated.
d. Romans viewed Christianity as a Jewish sect for its first two centuries.

108. Which of the following was a major cause of the Great Depression of the 1930s?

a. The overproduction and underconsumption of consumer goods
b. The failure of industry to produce sufficient consumer goods
c. Underproduction and rising prices in the agricultural sector
d. The reduction of import tariffs

109. The concept of checks and balances is evident in which of the following?

a. Federal judiciary appeals
b. Presidential veto
c. States' rights
d. The House and the Senate

110. What is the most common type of volcano on Earth?

a. Lava dome
b. Composite volcano
c. Shield volcano
d. Cinder cone

111. Of the following statements, which is true about the March on Versailles during the French Revolution?

a. The March on Versailles was an action undertaken by equal numbers of both men and women.
b. The March on Versailles was an action undertaken primarily by women.
c. The March on Versailles happened prior to the storming of the Bastille.
d. The March on Versailles was not effective in accomplishing its purpose.

112. What judicial system did America borrow from England?

a. Due process
b. Federal law
c. Commerce law
d. Common law

113. Who established the precedent for the two-term limit for the US presidency?

a. Abraham Lincoln
b. Alexander Hamilton
c. George Washington
d. Thomas Jefferson

114. How do animals of the phylum Mollusca respire?

a. Through gills
b. Through a trachea
c. Through book lungs
d. Through muscle contraction

115. A pulley lifts a 10-kg object 10 m into the air in 5 minutes. Using this information, you can calculate which of the following?

a. Mechanical advantage
b. Efficiency
c. Frictional resistance
d. Power

116. Two companion models, gradualism and punctuated equilibrium, dominate evolutionary theory. Which of the following statements is most consistent with the theory of punctuated equilibrium?

a. Fossils show changes over large periods of time.
b. Fossils showing intermediate characteristics may not necessarily be found.
c. Speciation occurs gradually.
d. Evolution is a slow, steady process.

Refer to the following for question 117:

The illustration below depicts the rock cycle. This cycle illustrates the fact that rocks are not unchanging entities; they undergo changes over time.

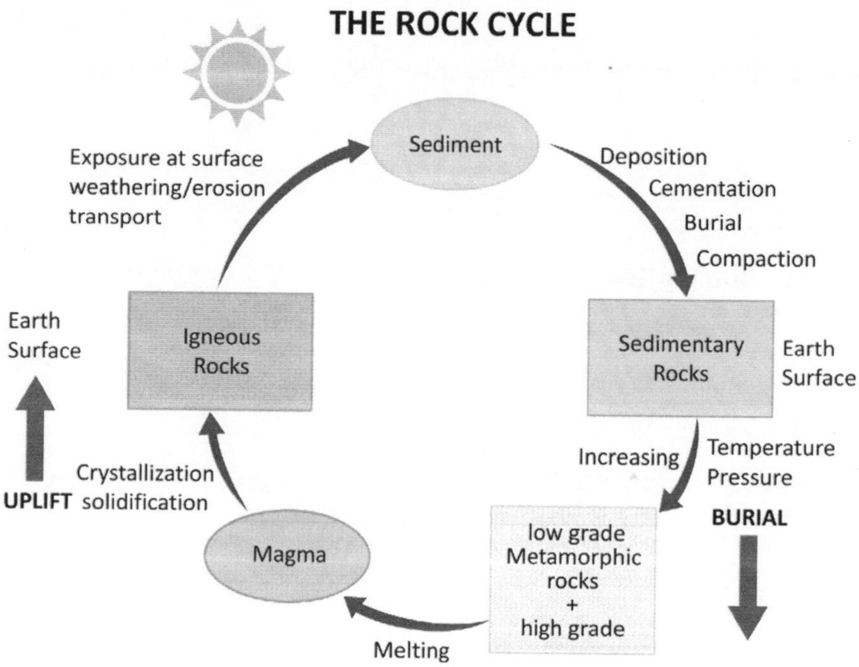

117. How are igneous rocks formed in the rock cycle?

a. Years of sediment are laid down on top of each other and forced together.
b. Acid rain caused by pollution creates holes in metamorphic rocks.
c. Dust and pebbles are pressed together underground from Earth's heat and pressure.
d. Magma from a volcanic eruption cools and hardens.

Refer to the following for question 118:

A biome featuring scrubby plants and small evergreen trees has a hot, dry summer followed by a wetter winter. The following food chain exists in the biome:

$$tree \rightarrow caterpillar \rightarrow frog \rightarrow snake \rightarrow hawk \rightarrow vulture \rightarrow worm$$

118. What trophic level contains the greatest amount of energy?

a. Tree
b. Caterpillar
c. Hawk
d. Worm

119. What happens to gas particles as temperature increases?

a. The average kinetic energy decreases while the intermolecular forces increase.
b. The average kinetic energy increases while the intermolecular forces decrease.
c. Both the average kinetic energy and the intermolecular forces decrease.
d. Both the average kinetic energy and the intermolecular forces increase.

120. Which of the following represents a chemical change?

a. Water sublimating
b. An apple turning brown
c. Salt dissolving in water
d. Rock being pulverized

121. What type of compound is formed by the combination of two or more nonmetallic elements with one another?

a. Organic
b. Ionic
c. Covalent
d. Chemical

122. Which of the following is an example of chemical weathering?

a. Rain freezing on the roadway
b. Ivy growing on the side of a wooden house
c. Vinegar fizzing when poured on a rock
d. A river carrying sediment downstream

123. Which of the following is an example of a descriptive study?

a. Comparing the average height of male vs female penguins of a particular species
b. Investigating the growth rate of fungi in various synthetic media
c. Testing the effectiveness of a drug with a double-blind study
d. Split-testing the impact on sales of a new description of menu items.

124. What happens to the temperature of a substance as it is changing phase from a liquid to a solid?

a. Its temperature increases due to the absorption of latent heat.
b. Its temperature decreases due to the heat of vaporization.
c. Its temperature decreases due to the latent heat of fusion.
d. Its temperature remains the same due to the latent heat of fusion.

125. Which of the following is NOT true of a chemical reaction?

a. Matter is neither gained nor lost.
b. Heat is absorbed or released.
c. The rate of the reaction increases with temperature.
d. The products have a different number of atoms than the reactants.

126. Fossils are least likely to be found in which type of rock?

a. Sedimentary rock
b. Metamorphic rock
c. Igneous rock
d. Fossils are commonly found in all types of rock

127. Which of the following statements correctly compares rocks and minerals?

a. Minerals may contain traces of organic compounds, while rocks do not.
b. Rocks are classified by their formation and the minerals they contain, while minerals are classified by their chemical composition and physical properties.
c. Both rocks and minerals can be polymorphs.
d. Both rocks and minerals may contain mineraloids.

128. Which of the following is true of different isotopes of the same element?

a. It has a different number of protons than its element.
b. It has a different number of electrons than its element.
c. It has a different charge as compared to its element.
d. It has a different number of neutrons than other isotopes of the same element.

129. Which action will help dissolve a gas in a liquid if the gas and liquid are placed in a sealed container?

a. Heat the liquid.
b. Cool the liquid.
c. Shake the container.
d. Decrease the pressure on the lid.

130. How does the freezing point of sea water compare to that of fresh water?

a. Sea water has a higher freezing point.
b. Sea water has a lower freezing point.
c. They are the same.
d. Sea water does not freeze.

131. Tropical climate zones are characterized by:

a. Extreme temperature variations between night and day
b. Extreme temperature variations between seasons
c. Frequent rainfall
d. All of the above

132. The process whereby a radioactive element releases energy slowly over a long period of time to lower its energy and become more stable is best described as which of the following?

a. Combustion
b. Fission
c. Fusion
d. Decay

133. This organelle contains digestive enzymes that break down food and unneeded substances. They are also thought to be linked to the aging process. What part of a cell does this describe?

a. Lysosomes
b. Chromatin
c. Plastids
d. Golgi apparatus

134. On a topographic map, an area where the contour lines are very close together indicates which of the following?

a. A stream is present.
b. The slope is very gentle.
c. The slope is very steep.
d. The area surrounds a depression.

135. The distance from the earth to the sun is equal to which of the following?

a. One astronomical unit
b. One light-year
c. One parsec
d. One arcsecond

136. Which of the following observations provides the best evidence that sound can travel through solid objects?

a. Sound waves cannot travel through a vacuum.
b. The atoms of a solid are packed tightly together.
c. If you knock on a solid object, it makes a sound.
d. You can hear a sound on the other side of a solid wall.

137. Which of the following divisions of plants produces seeds for reproduction?

a. Anthophyta
b. Lycophyta
c. Sphenophyta
d. Pterophyta

138. Which of the following creates a magnetic field?

a. The spinning and rotating of electrons in atoms
b. The separation of charged particles in atoms
c. The vibrational and translational motion of atoms
d. Loosely held valence electrons surrounding an atom

139. The asteroid belt in our solar system is located between:

a. Earth and Mars
b. Neptune and Pluto
c. Uranus and Saturn
d. Mars and Jupiter

140. In a parallel circuit, there are three paths: A, B, and C. Path A has a resistance of 10 ohms, path B a resistance of 5 ohms, and path C a resistance of 2 ohms. How do the voltage and current change for each path?

a. Voltage and current are kept the same in each path.
b. Voltage is greatest in path A and current is greatest in path C.
c. Voltage is lowest in path C and current is greatest in path C.
d. Voltage is the same for each path and current is greatest in path C.

141. Which of the following is not an advantage angiosperms show over other types of plants?

a. Larger leaves
b. Double fertilization
c. Dormant seeds
d. Lower seed dispersal

142. Visual literacy can best be described as which of the following?

a. The ability to communicate through images and comprehend the messages contained in images
b. The ability to construct three-dimensional images
c. The incorporation of literary text into works of art
d. The incorporation of art into literary texts

143. Which of the following tempos is played between 120 and 168 beats per minute?

a. Presto
b. Moderato
c. Allegro
d. Largo

144. In order for a pigment to reach the desired consistency for fluid painting, with which of the following should it NOT be combined?

a. Turpentine
b. Fresco
c. A tempera
d. An oil medium

145. What are the threads that are stretched taut across the loom before weaving begins called?

a. Warp
b. Weft
c. Loom
d. Twill

146. According to research studies, what is true about the impact of physical activity (PA) on health risks?

a. PA lowers heart disease, stroke, diabetes, and colon and breast cancer risks.
b. PA reduces risks of heart disease and stroke but not of diabetes or any cancer.
c. PA reduces risks of all these diseases, but amounts of PA needed for each disease vary greatly.
d. PA in adequate amounts improves overall well-being but does not lower disease risks.

147. Which of the following composers is MOST strongly associated with the Romantic Period?

a. Johann Sebastian Bach
b. Maurice Ravel
c. Aaron Copland
d. Johannes Brahms

148. Which of the following artistic elements is primarily associated with three-dimensional works such as sculpture or decorative arts?

a. Line
b. Form
c. Proportion
d. Balance

149. By correctly rendering proportion in her work, an artist can create which of the following artistic effects?

a. Emotion
b. Energy
c. Realism
d. Rhythm

150. The purpose of an artist portfolio is MOST often to

a. demonstrate an artist's capabilities.
b. communicate past work history and education.
c. teach an artist's students.
d. include all artwork for copyright purposes.

Answer Key and Explanations for Test #1

1. B: Researchers have found that the writing process both forms a hierarchy and is observably recursive. Moreover, they find that when students continually revise their writing, they are able to consider new ideas and to incorporate these ideas into their work. Therefore, choice B is correct. Students who are rewriting and revising do not merely correct mechanical errors (A); they also add to the content and quality of their writing. Furthermore, research shows that writers (including students) not only revise their actual writing during rewrites, but they also reconsider their original writing goals rather than always retaining them (C), and they revisit their prewriting plans rather than leaving these unaffected (D).

2. C: Once the students' notecards have been checked and edited for accuracy, they can easily be used to demonstrate the process of organizing ideas in an essay or research paper. Students can use their notecards as aids for making their outlines. They simply have to arrange the notecards in an appropriate order and add pertinent information to bridge the ideas together in their writing.

3. D: Fluent readers are able to read smoothly and comfortably at a steady pace (rate). The more quickly a child reads, the greater the chance of leaving out a word or substituting one word for another (for example, *sink* instead of *shrink*). Fluent readers are able to maintain accuracy without sacrificing rate. Fluent readers also stress important words in a text, group words into rhythmic phrases, and read with intonation (prosody).

4. C: Homophones are words that are pronounced the same but differ in meaning. For example, a bride wears a 2-carat ring, but a horse eats a carrot. These words are not all nouns or monosyllabic, and none of them are diphthongs. Diphthongs (D) are a single-syllable sound made up by combining two vowels, such as in the words *weird*, *applause*, and *boy*.

5. A: It is a standard of Information Literacy that students must use their own critical thinking skills to evaluate the quality of the information and its sources before they use it, so choice A is correct. Another standard of Information Literacy is that the student should ascertain how much information he or she needs before seeking out the information, as identifying what information is necessary after uncovering excessive information is inefficient (B). Instead of acquiring as much information as possible, students should determine how much information is needed to achieve a reasonable goal. An additional Information Literacy standard is to access necessary information in an efficient and effective way. However, none of these standards include the idea that students will sacrifice any incidental learning by being efficient in their accessing of information, so choice C is incorrect. Another part of Information Literacy Standards is the principle that students should use the information they find in ways that are effective for their specific purposes; this does not require that students avoid using information for purposes that it was not meant to serve, so choice D is incorrect.

6. B: Spelling is often taught in a systematic way. Students receive words and memorize them for quizzes and tests. However, spelling is related to many aspects of language and must be treated as a dynamic subject. Integrating the words into other parts of language instruction will help students not only learn how to spell correctly, but also to recall meanings of words and various rules of English spelling and grammar. By using the same words in different subjects, the students will retain the information more readily than if they study the words intensely for one week in only one context.

7. C: Tier-two words are words that are used with high frequency across a variety of disciplines or words with multiple meanings. They are characteristic of mature language users. Knowing these words is crucial to attaining an acceptable level of reading comprehension and communication skills.

8. D: Teachers will observe a variety of developmental arcs when teaching reading, since all students learn differently. It is very important to understand which instances are normal in the course of learning and which signal a learning difficulty. Barrett is still exhibiting confusion over certain letter-sounds, typically when the letters look similar. At his age, this difficulty could suggest that Barrett has an issue with reading that could be addressed by a reading specialist. The other three choices describe normal behaviors that are commonly exhibited by children when they are learning to read. Choice C, Noelle, may describe an instance in which a student is having a learning problem. However, the teacher will need more information about Noelle's reading skills besides her reluctance to read before making a determination about how to proceed.

9. C: The MLA guidelines for citing sources in research papers advise that multiple authors of the same work can be cited in in-text citations by using the first author's name plus *et al*, where *et al* refers to all the other authors. However, this convention is only advised for situations where there are three or more authors, so choice C is correct. The guidelines also say that in cases where there are two or three authors, each author should be named in a serial list, either in a signal phrase or in a parenthetical reference. For example, authors Smith and Jones could be cited with "Smith and Jones note that ... (45)" or "(Smith and Jones 45)," and authors Smith, Jones, and Gray could be cited with "Smith, Jones, and Gray note that ... (45)" or simply "(Smith, Jones, and Gray 45)." Therefore, choices A, B, and D are incorrect.

10. A: The /p/ sound is among the earliest phonemes to develop, from ages 1.5 to 3 years old. The /ʒ/ phoneme (B) has the oldest age norm for normal development—5.5 years to 8.5 years old is a typical range for children to acquire correct production of this sound. The /v/ sound (C) typically develops in most children from the ages of 4 to 8 years. Most children develop correct articulation of the /s/ sound (D) by 2.5 to 4 years old. Hence, not all kindergarteners, who are typically around 5 years old, are expected to master phonemes with acquisition norm ranges older than 5-8 years. A 5-year-old is most likely to be referred for SLP evaluation if s/he does not correctly produce /p/, which children normally develop by around 3 years old.

11. B: Prior knowledge, which rises from experience and previous learning, provides a framework by which new knowledge gained from the act of reading can be integrated. Every act of reading enriches a student's store of prior knowledge and increases that student's future ability to comprehend more fully any new knowledge acquired through reading.

12. B: Writing haikus will promote students' vocabularies. The tightly controlled syllabic requirements will cause students to search for words outside their normal vocabularies that will fit the rigid framework and still express the writer's intended meanings. Often, students will rediscover a word whose meaning they know, but they don't often use.

13. A: Mnemonic devices are a way to aid in memorization. The concept to be memorized is linked to a device: an easily remembered song, saying, or image. To remember the concept, one needs only to remember the device.

14. A: While there is no consensus among experts as to any universal sequence of instruction for teaching the alphabetic principle through phonics instruction, they do agree that, to enable children to start reading words as soon as possible, the highest-utility relationships should be introduced earliest. For example, the letters *m, a, p, t,* and *s* are all used frequently, whereas the *x* in *box*, the sound of *ey* in *they*, and the letter *a* when pronounced as it is in *want* have lower-utility letter-sound correspondences. Important considerations for the alphabetic principle are to teach letter-sound correspondences in isolation, not in word contexts; to teach them explicitly; to give students opportunities to practice letter-sound relationships within their other daily lessons, not only separately; and to include cumulative reviews of relationships taught earlier along with new ones in practice opportunities.

15. A: Letter–sound correspondence relies on the relationship between a spoken sound or group of sounds and the letters conventionally used in English to write them.

16. A: Explicit instruction involves clarifying the goal, modeling strategies, and offering explanations geared to a student's level of understanding. Explicit instruction is well organized and structured. It offers easily understood steps and depends in part on frequent reference to previously learned materials.

17. C: *Diction* refers to the overall choice of language a writer or speaker makes. *Jargon* is a specialized terminology, used in a discipline, that is not readily understood by readers outside of that discipline. Choice C fills in the blanks correctly. *Style* (A and D) refers to the effect a writer achieves through language. It encompasses diction, which encompasses word choice. *Vocabulary* (D) refers to any set of words in a language.

18. B: Students must be able to distinguish between printed words and the spaces between them to identify the first and last letters of each word, as spaces are the boundaries between words. It is not true that all normally developing students can tell words from spaces: those not exposed to or familiar with print media may need to be taught this distinction. Although left-to-right directionality is more of a problem for ELL students whose L1s have different writing or printing directions (e.g., some Asian languages are written vertically, some can be written vertically or horizontally, and some Semitic languages like Hebrew and Arabic are written right-to-left), again, children unfamiliar with print or writing may also not know writing, print, or book directionality either. Identifying basic punctuation is important to reading comprehension as it affects meaning. For example, consider "Let's eat, Grandma" vs. "Let's eat Grandma"—one comma differentiates an invitation to dinner from a cannibalistic proposal.

19. A: At the beginning of the school year, second-grade students should be able to read 50–80 words per minute. By the time they are well into the school year, second-grade level reading is tracked at 85 words per minute.

20. A: Teachers of English language learners should not employ idioms and slang in their instruction because these informal uses of speech are likely to confuse the students. Involving students in hands-on activities such as group reading and language play makes the experience both more meaningful and more immediate. New knowledge can only be absorbed by attaching it to prior knowledge; referencing what students already know is essential. Speaking slowly to English language learners is important, because they are processing what is being said at a slower rate than a native speaker.

21. A: Choice A is correct as evaluation (i.e., making critical judgments about some information) commonly incorporates the processes that the other answer choices refer to and is therefore more complex than they are. Application (B) requires taking information learned and using it in new or different circumstances. Comprehension (C) requires showing understanding of the information learned. Knowledge recall (D) involves showing proficiency in information learned.

22. D: To instruct students in word analysis following a sequence progressing from simpler to more complex, teachers would first introduce individual phonemes (speech sounds); then the blending of two or more individual phonemes; then onsets and rimes (i.e., phonograms and word families) such as *-ack*, *-ide*, *-ay*, *-ight*, *-ine*, etc.; then the easier short vowels, followed by the more difficult long vowels; then blends of individual consonants; then CVC (consonant-vowel-consonant) words (e.g., *bag*, *hot*, *red*, *sit*) and other common patterns of consonants and vowels in words; and then the six most common types of syllables (i.e., closed, VCe, open, vowel team, *r*-controlled, and C-*le*).

23. C: Students can easily become bored or disinterested in reading if they are not exposed to a variety of reading texts. Also, reading can be overwhelming or frustrating for students who are still learning to read fluently or to comprehend what they read. By incorporating media, oral stories, and various types of print, students of all ability levels can build both fluency and comprehension skills. This approach also enables the teacher and students to discuss the relationship between all aspects of literacy—including speaking, listening, thinking, viewing, and reading.

24. B: Coarticulation affects phonemic awareness. Vocalizing words involves arranging a series of continuous, voiced, unvoiced, and stop sounds. As one sound is being uttered, the tongue and lips are already assuming the shape required by the next sound in the word. This process, which is not conscious, can distort individual sounds. One sound can slur into another, clip the end of the previous sound, or flatten or heighten a sound. For children who have difficulty hearing distinct phonemic sounds, individual instruction may be required.

25. B: This prompt focuses not only on reading fluency skills, but also on the issue of the young reader's confidence. It is very common for students who feel unsuccessful at reading to avoid the skill altogether. The teacher in this question realizes something important: it is vital to build a student's confidence with reading as he or she builds skill. In choice A there is a faulty assumption that a student could ever memorize enough words to eliminate the need to decode. While some students with processing disorders or different learning styles do rely more heavily on sight words, this practice should not be solely relied upon. In choice C the students will likely feel negatively about being asked to read young children's books; their lack of confidence may be reinforced by this plan. In choice D students may also be frustrated by the extra work they are required to do without any evidence of success with this practice. In choice B, students can build their fluency skills by creating words with various sounds, which is often easier for students than decoding as they are learning to read. As their knowledge of letter-sound relationships grows, they will become better at decoding words they see on the page. Allowing students to encode will also provide them with more chances to feel successful as they learn.

26. B: Identifying point of view (A) is an example of literal reading comprehension. Explaining the point of view (B) is an example of evaluative reading comprehension. Identifying the main idea of a text passage (C) is an example of literal reading comprehension. Making predictions about what will happen in a text (D) is an example of inferential reading comprehension.

27. C: Signal words give the reader hints about the purpose of a particular passage. Some signal words are concerned with comparing/contrasting, some with cause and effect, some with temporal sequencing, some with physical location, and some with a problem and its solution. The words since, therefore, and accordingly are words used when describing an outcome; outcomes have causes.

28. B: Semantics is the branch of linguistics that deals with meaning. The semantic system in language includes all aspects of language use that carries meaning. Semantics include words, phrases, sentences, and further contexts that help to convey meaning. Semantics are involved in both receptive and expressive language processes. Choice A is incorrect because the graphophonic system is largely related to the sounds of a language and their written representations. Graphophonics study the relationship between phonics and orthography (writing system). Choice C is incorrect because the syntactic system refers primarily to sentence structure, word order, and other elements of grammar. Syntax does impact meaning, but in a more indirect way than semantics. Choice D is incorrect because pragmatics refers to practical application of language in a variety of contexts. For example, pragmatics is interested in language shifts between social and academic contexts. In reading, this involves being aware of how writers use language to convey moods and draw out more subtle implications.

29. B: There are many different adults who can assist children in acquiring various types of language. If a child inconsistently mispronounces certain sounds in reading, he or she may simply need a reminder or instruction from a teacher. Often, children will not acquire knowledge of certain letters or sounds until a certain age. However, the child in this scenario mispronounces words consistently both in reading and in conversation. This combination suggests that the child is not physically able to make certain speech sounds. A speech-language pathologist can assist in determining whether or not the child's mispronunciations indicate the need for therapy. A speech pathologist can also work directly with the child to help him or her learn how to make certain sounds.

30. B: Indirect ways in which students receive instruction and learn vocabulary include through daily conversations, reading on their own, and being read aloud to by adults. Direct instruction and learning in vocabulary include teachers providing extended instruction exposing students repeatedly to vocabulary words in multiple teaching contexts, teachers pre-teaching specific words found in text prior to students reading it, and teachers instructing students over extended time periods and having them actively work with vocabulary words.

31. C: Analogizing is based on recognizing the pattern of letters in words that share phonological and orthographical similarities. In phonology and in spelling, the initial sound of a word is called an *onset*, whereas the sounds that follow the onset are called the *rime*. The following words each have a different onset sound, but share the same rime: *rent*, *sent*, *bent*, and *dent*. Rime analogies are an explicit teaching method that helps draw attention to patterns in rime and onset spellings. As students become more familiar with these patterns, they should be able to decode common rime patterns in words faster and with greater accuracy, contributing to higher reading fluency.

32. A: The student making this observation is connecting a reading about mythological gods to the world—in this instance, to human nature—by noting that despite greater powers, the gods' emotional reactions and behaviors are like those of humans. Since this is an example of connecting text to what the student knows about the world choice A is correct. The student statements in choices B and D reflect connections of text to text—fiction (a novel) to historical accounts of a period, and a character description to another story with a similar character. The student statement in option C reflects a connection of text to self; the student can relate to the feelings of a character in the text.

33. B: Reading responses can take various forms. The most common form of reading response is likely to be targeted student writing. Students may use journals, worksheets, or other formats to construct written responses to something they have read. The purpose of this type of assignment can range from fostering an appreciation of written text to helping a student prepare for an activity in class. Students may also engage in creating an oral reading response in the form of a presentation or debate. Ultimately, reading response increases a student's capacity to understand what is read and to analyze personal responses to the text.

34. C: Depending on their type, graphs can be used to compare quantities or values at the same point in time (or irrespective of time), or to show changes in quantities or values over time. For example, a bar graph can show different numbers of students in different categories or different test scores next to each other for comparison, or different numbers presented yearly, monthly, weekly, daily, etc. Line graphs only show changes in values over time. Tables are good for organizing information into categories but do not show linear changes over time. Maps, when cartographic (actual maps), depict geographical locations and can include other information (e.g., population totals, percentages, income, domestic or national product figures, annual rainfall, temperatures) via color-coding and other graphics. Other map types used in education, including concept maps for students, curriculum maps and resource maps for educators, etc., do not show linear chronological change. Charts like pie charts, which show percentages or proportions of a whole quantity divided by categories, do not show change over time.

35. C: By considering the other words in the story, the student can determine the missing words. The student is depending on the information supplied by the rest of the story. This information puts the story into context.

36. C: Second languages can be learned in a number of educational contexts. For example, they can be segregated from the L1, formally taught via the medium of the L1, taught through submersion, or taught within the language classroom but not used to communicate outside of it. The L2 can also be learned in several natural contexts. Because of these variations, L2 learners may acquire different elements of the language or may vary in how much of the language they acquire, so choice C is correct. Just like an L2, an L1 can also be learned in an education or natural context, so choice A is incorrect. While many L1s are learned naturally at first, they are learned in educational contexts as well, so choice B is incorrect. Just like L1s, L2s can be learned and used naturally, so choice D is incorrect.

37. B: In this project, students will engage in almost every aspect of literacy in a group context. Students must first accurately read and comprehend a short play; they will also use their writing skills to adapt the play to their specific purposes by cutting or adding text. The teacher can gauge the students' interpretive skills by the way they perform their play. By splitting the students into groups, the teacher can provide each student the chance to interpret and perform, as well as to experience the performances. Audience members receive additional practice with listening and interpreting when they generate responses to the performances. Group members can evaluate the effectiveness of their performances based on responses from the audience.

38. D: Teachers should instruct students in writing not in isolation, not relating writing only to reading or reading and speaking, but by showing students the interrelationships of listening, speaking, reading, and writing. In addition, teachers should not just teach writing as a rote chore or drill, but give students lessons and assignments that demonstrate legitimate purposes for writing and provide topics to write about that are meaningful to students.

39. C: Until the teacher monitors the child's verbal abilities and habits, she cannot determine if the lack of interaction suggests a learning disability, an emotional problem, or simply a shy personality. The teacher should informally observe the child over a period of time, noting if and when she initiates or responds to oral language, if she is reading with apparent comprehension, if her vocabulary is limited, and the degree to which the child is interested in understanding.

40. C: The root of the modern English word *debt* is the Latin word *debitum*, which is also the source of the *b*, so choice C is correct. Early scribes and printers, described by some as "inkhorn scholars," introduced many silent letters to English spellings to indicate their Latin or Greek roots, as in this case. Since the origin of the word is in Latin and not Greek, choice B is incorrect. The word came into English during the Middle English form of the language. Therefore, it did not exist in Old English, so choice C is incorrect, and it was not originally a Middle English word, so choice D is incorrect.

41. C: Literacy skills are various and include a number of different sub-skills: reading fluency, comprehension, application of knowledge, listening, speaking, grammar, spelling, writing, and more. It is important for teachers to track student development for lesson design and to communicate with the student, future teachers, and parents. Therefore, it is best to keep samples of a variety of assessments, including descriptions of reading fluency, writing samples, projects, and formal assessments of grammar, spelling, and other skills. All of these skills develop simultaneously, but at different rates. Therefore, it is impossible to judge a student's literacy based only on one measure of assessment.

42. C: When teaching students about various media types, the four categories listed as choices are ways to classify them. One-on-one communication media includes emails, phone calls, and letters but not books. Entertainment media includes movies, TV shows, and video games; novels are included, but not the wider class of books. (Note that there are many more kinds of books than novels.) Informative media includes books, newspapers, websites, and radio news broadcasts. Persuasive media includes advertising, direct mail marketing, telemarketing calls, and infomercials.

43. A: The student should receive instruction focused on just the areas in which he is exhibiting difficulty, which are comprehension and vocabulary. Improved vocabulary will give him greater skill at comprehending the meaning of a particular text. Strategies focused on enhancing comprehension together with a stronger vocabulary will provide the greatest help.

44. D: This is an example of a compound-complex sentence, so choice D is correct. The other choices are incorrect, as they refer to different sentence types. A simple (A) sentence contains no more than one independent clause (i.e., a subject and a finite verb) and no dependent clauses. Its subject and verb may be compound (e.g., "John and Mary" as the subject, or "comes and goes" as the verb). A complex (B) sentence contains an independent clause and one or more dependent clauses. Dependent clauses are joined to independent clauses or other dependent clauses by subordinating conjunctions (as in "after she left") or relative pronouns (as in "that he had never heard"). A compound (C) sentence contains two or more independent clauses. The compound-complex sentence, as its name implies, combines both compound and complex sentence structures. It combines more than one independent clause with at least one dependent clause. In the example sentence given, the first two clauses, joined by "however," are independent, and the clause modifying "actual test questions," beginning with "which cover," is a relative, dependent clause.

45. A: The words in this question prompt are most often used to refer to *sounds* made while reading. Initial/onset, medial, and final sounds are decoded in the beginning, middle, and end of words. When a teacher needs to assess an emergent or struggling reader's ability to differentiate between sounds in words, he or she may use a phonological awareness assessment. This tool will provide the teacher with information about the student's current ability to decode or encode words.

46. B: One set of criteria suggested for use with informal reading inventories (Pumfrey, 1976) equates the independent reading level to knowing 95-100 percent of words in isolation, 99-100 percent accuracy reading words in context, and answering comprehension questions 90-100 percent correctly; the instructional level to knowing 60-94 percent of words in isolation, 95-98 percent accuracy reading words in context, and answering comprehension questions 70-89 percent correctly; and the frustration level with knowing below 50 percent of words in isolation, reading below 95 percent of words accurately in context, and answering below 70 percent of comprehension questions correctly. Hence, the text described is at the student's frustration level and too difficult.

47. A: A phoneme is a unit of language that represents the smallest unit of sound. For instance, the *k* in *kit* or the *ph* in *graph* both represent English phonemes. Graphemes are written phonemes and can be alphabetic letters, numbers, characters, punctuation marks, and so on. Neither phonemes nor graphemes have semantic meaning unless they are used as part of a larger unit of language, such as the morpheme. Morphemes can be roots, prefixes, and suffixes. The word *rechargeable* is comprised of three morphemes: *re*, *charge*, and *able*. Each component of this word has a meaning unto itself, but when combined with the others, each one is used to make a new word with a new meaning.

48. D: The expression $(x-2)^2$ may be expanded as x^2-4x+4. Multiplication of $-3x$ by this expression gives $-3x^3+12x^2-12x$.

49. B: The sequence $\frac{1}{5}\frac{1}{25}\frac{1}{125}\frac{1}{625}$ ... may be used to represent the situation. Substituting the initial value of $\frac{1}{5}$ and the common ratio of $\frac{1}{5}$ into the formula $S=\frac{a}{1-r}$:

$$S=\frac{\frac{1}{5}}{1-\frac{1}{5}}=\frac{\frac{1}{5}}{\frac{4}{5}}=\frac{1}{4}$$

50. A: The net of a triangular prism has three rectangular faces and two triangular faces, and the rectangular faces must all be able to connect to each other directly. This is shown in choice A.

51. B: Since they are not mutually exclusive events, $P(4\text{ or }E)=P(4)+P(E)-P(4\text{ and }E)$. Substituting the probability of each event gives $P(4\text{ or }E)=\frac{1}{6}+\frac{1}{2}-\frac{1}{6}=\frac{1}{2}$.

52. A: Choice A is correct because second grade students should be able to calculate how money saved can accumulate into a larger amount over time. Choice D, which is expected of first grade students, is too basic for second grade. Choice C is expected of third grade students. Choice B is expected of fifth grade students. Therefore, the correct choice is A.

53. B: Use the order of operations to find the value for this expression. The order of operations is: parentheses, exponents, multiplication and division, addition and subtraction.

$$\begin{aligned}&-3\times 5^2+2(4-18)+33\\&=-3\times 5^2+2(-14)+33\\&=-3\times 25+2(-14)+33\\&=-75+(-28)+33\\&=-70\end{aligned}$$

The value of the expression is -70.

54. B: Claus has \$20 to spend, so the amount he spends must be less than or equal to ($\leq$) \$20. The entrance fee of \$2.50 is only charged once, so it should not be multiplied by x. The cost of a ticket multiplied by x represents the cost of buying x tickets. The entrance fee plus the cost of the tickets is Claus's total cost: $2.50+2x\leq 20$.

55. A: Since area is two dimensional, the units for area have an exponent of 2, such as in^2, yd^2, cm^2, or m^2. Choice B includes a unit of length (yd) and a unit of volume (yd^3). Choice C includes only units of length. Choice C includes a square unit of time (s^2). Therefore, the correct choice is A.

56. B: Since the events are mutually exclusive, the sum of their individual probabilities is 1.0. Subtracting 0.6 from 1.0 yields 0.4. Therefore, the correct choice is B.

57. A: The teacher is using a concrete representation of the concept in question, since the dice she is using are physical objects which help communicate the concept. Verbal, graphic, and pictorial are not correct since the student is not merely observing a discussion about the concept or looking at a graphic representation. Concrete representations often lead to more depth of knowledge and better retention of the concepts.

58. D: We can use the table to find the linear equation in slope-intercept form, $y = mx + b$, where m is the slope and b is the y-intercept. The table shows the y-intercept (the y-value at $x = 0$) to be −5. The slope is the ratio of the change in y-values to the corresponding change in x-values. As the x-value increases by 1, the y-value increases by 3. Thus, the slope is $\frac{3}{1}$, or 3. So the equation is $y = 3x - 5$.

Only the graphs in choices B and D have a y-intercept at −5. Of these two graphs, only choice D has a y-value increase of 3 for each x-value increase of 1, indicating a slope of 3.

59. C: A line segment with endpoints (x_1, y_1) and (x_2, y_2) has the midpoint $\left(\frac{x_1+x_2}{2}, \frac{y_1+y_2}{2}\right)$. The line segment shown has endpoints (1,2) and (8,8), so its midpoint is $\left(\frac{1+8}{2}, \frac{2+8}{2}\right)$, or (4.5,5).

60. D: The perimeter of the triangle is equal to the sum of the side lengths. The length of the longer diagonal side may be represented as $d = \sqrt{(4-1)^2 + (5-2)^2}$, which simplifies to $d = \sqrt{18}$. The length of the shorter diagonal side may be represented as $d = \sqrt{(6-4)^2 + (2-5)^2}$, which simplifies to $d = \sqrt{13}$. The base length is 5 units. Thus, the perimeter is equal to $5 + \sqrt{18} + \sqrt{13}$, which is approximately 12.85 units. Since each unit represents 5 miles, the total distance she will have walked is equal to the product of 12.85 and 5, or approximately 64 miles.

61. B: The slope of a straight line is a vital concept to understanding linear equations.

62. C: The expression representing the monthly charge for Company A is $25 + 0.05m$, where m is the time in minutes spent talking on the phone. Set this expression equal to the monthly charge for Company B, which is $50. Solve for m to find the number of minutes the two companies charge the same amount.

$$\begin{aligned} \$25 + \$0.05m &= \$50 \\ \$0.05m &= \$25 \\ m &= 500 \end{aligned}$$

Notice that the answer choices are given in hours, not in minutes. Since there are 60 minutes in an hour, $m = \frac{500}{60}$ hours $= 8\frac{1}{3}$ hours. One-third of an hour is 20 minutes, so m is 8 hours and 20 minutes.

63. C: A system of linear equations can be solved by using matrices or by using the graphing, substitution, or elimination (also called linear combination) method. The elimination method is shown here:

$$3x + 4y = 2$$
$$2x + 6y = -2$$

In order to eliminate x by linear combination, multiply the top equation by 2 and the bottom equation by –3 so that the coefficients of the x-terms will be additive inverses.

$$2(3x + 4y = 2)$$
$$-3(2x + 6y = -2)$$

Then, add the two equations and solve for y.

$$\begin{aligned} 6x + 8y &= 4 \\ \underline{-6x - 18y} &\underline{= 6} \\ -10y &= 10 \\ y &= -1 \end{aligned}$$

Substitute –1 for y in either of the given equations and solve for x.

$$\begin{aligned} 3x + 4y &= 2 \\ 3x + 4(-1) &= 2 \\ 3x - 4 &= 2 \\ 3x &= 6 \\ x &= 2 \end{aligned}$$

The solution to the system of equations is $(2, -1)$.

64. D: The cross-section is a hexagon.

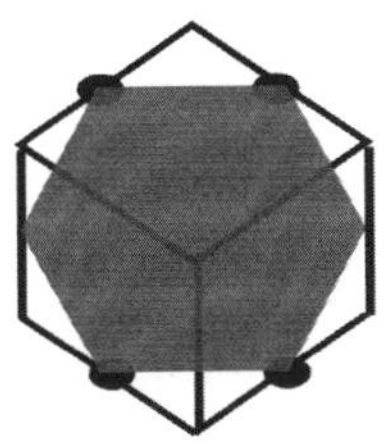

65. D: Since there are 100 homes' market times represented in each set, the median time a home spends on the market is between the 50th and 51st data point in each set. The 50th and 51st data points for Zip Code 1 are six months and seven months, respectively, so the median time a house in Zip Code 1 spends on the market is between six and seven months (6.5 months), which by the realtor's definition of market time is a seven-month market time. The 50th and 51st data points for Zip Code 2 are both thirteen months, so the median time a house in Zip Code 2 spends on the market is thirteen months. Therefore, there is a six-month difference between the median of Zip Code 1 and the median of Zip Code 2.

To find the mean market time for 100 houses, find the sum of the market times and divide by 100. If the frequency of a one-month market time is 9, the number 1 is added nine times (1×9), if the frequency of a two-month market time is 10, the number 2 is added ten times (2×10), and so on. So, to find the average market time, divide by 100 the sum of the products of each market time and its corresponding frequency. For Zip Code 1, the mean market time is 7.38 months, which, by the realtor's definition of market time, is an eight-month market time. For Zip Code 2, the mean market time is 12.74, which, by the realtor's definition of market time, is a thirteen-month market time. Therefore, the difference between the mean of Zip Code 1 and the mean of Zip Code 2 is 5 months.

The mode market time is the market time for which the frequency is the highest. For Zip Code 1, the mode market time is three months, and for Zip Code 2, the mode market time is eleven months. Therefore, the median time a house spends on the market in Zip Code 1 is less than the mean time a house spends on the market in Zip Code 1.

66. C: The amount he donates is equal to 1% of $45,000. To calculate this value, multiply the two numbers. To multiply a percentage by another number, first convert the percentage to a decimal by changing the percentage sign to a decimal point and moving the decimal point two places to the left. Therefore, $1\% = 0.01$. Now the two numbers can be multiplied: $0.01 \times \$45{,}000 = 1 \times \$450 = \$450$. Thus, he donates $450.

67. D: This situation may be modeled by an arithmetic sequence, with a common difference of 4 and an initial value of 3. Substituting the common difference and initial value into the formula, $a_n = a_1 + (n-1)d$, gives $a_n = 3 + (n-1)(4)$, which simplifies to $a_n = 4n - 1$.

68. B: The following proportion may be written and solved for x: $\frac{15\text{ ft}}{5\text{ ft}} = \frac{6\text{ ft}}{x\text{ ft}}$. Cross multiplying results in $15x = 30$. Dividing by 15 gives $x = 2$. Thus, the shadow cast by the man is 2 feet in length.

69. C: The probability of tossing a coin and getting heads is $\frac{1}{2}$. Multiply the probability by the number of coin tosses: $\frac{1}{2} \times 300 = 150$. You would expect to get heads about 150 times.

70. B: Since Mr. Mancelli has eight candy bars, he can make at most eight identical bags, each containing a single candy bar and a single package of gum; in this case, however, he will have four packages of gum remaining. To determine the greatest number of prize bags he can make so that no candy bars or packages of gum remain, he needs to find the largest number of groups that both 8 and 12 can be split into. In other words, he must find the greatest common divisor (or greatest common factor) of 8 and 12. The factors of 8 are 1, 2, 4, and 8. The factors of 12 are 1, 2, 3, 4, 6, and 12. The greatest common divisor of 8 and 12 is 4. He can make four prize bags, each of which contains two candy bars and three packages of gum. Therefore, the correct choice is B.

71. C: Addition and subtraction of whole numbers up to 20 using concrete and pictorial models and number sentences is the appropriate level for first-grade students. Numbers up to 1,000 and number pairs are appropriate for third-grade students. Counting by ones and tens is appropriate for kindergarten.

72. A: A hexagon has six sides. A hexagonal prism has 8 faces consisting of two hexagonal bases and six rectangular lateral faces. This results in 18 edges and 12 vertices. Therefore, the correct choice is A.

73. D: The theoretical probability of tossing any particular number is $\frac{1}{6}$. Since she tosses a two $\frac{3}{12}$, or $\frac{1}{4}$ times, the experimental probability of tossing a 2 is greater than the theoretical probability. The experimental probability should grow closer to the experimental probability as she tosses the die more times.

74. C: Substitute 2 for each x and simplify.

$$f(2) = \frac{(2)^3 - 2(2) + 1}{3(2)} = \frac{8 - 4 + 1}{6} = \frac{5}{6}$$

75. C: The distance may be calculated using the distance formula, $d = \sqrt{(x_2 - x_1)^2 + (y_2 - y_1)^2}$. Substitute the given coordinates into the formula.

$$d = \sqrt{\left(4 - (-8)\right)^2 + (3 - 6)^2}$$
$$d = \sqrt{(12)^2 + (-3)^2}$$
$$d = \sqrt{144 + 9}$$
$$d = \sqrt{153}$$

Therefore, the distance between the two points is $\sqrt{153}$.

76. B: $A \cup B$ means "A union B," or all of the elements in either of the two sets. "A union B" represents "A or B," that is, an element is in the union of A and B if it is in A *or* it is in B. The elements in sets A or B are 9, 4, -3, 8, 6, 0, -4, and 2.

77. D: Since there are 100 cm in a meter, on a 1 : 100 scale drawing, each centimeter represents one meter. Therefore, an area of one square centimeter on the drawing represents one square meter in actuality. Since the area of the room in the scale drawing is 30 cm^2, the room's actual area is 30 m^2.

Another way to determine the area of the room is to write and solve an equation, such as this one: $\frac{l}{100} \times \frac{w}{100} = 30\ \text{cm}^2$, where l and w are the dimensions of the actual room.

$$\frac{lw}{10{,}000} = 30\ \text{cm}^2$$
$$\text{Area} = 300{,}000\ \text{cm}^2$$

Since this is not one of the answer choices, convert cm^2 to m^2.

$$300{,}000\ \text{cm}^2 \times \frac{1\ \text{m}}{100\ \text{cm}} \times \frac{1\ \text{m}}{100\ \text{cm}} = 30\ \text{m}^2$$

78. C: If l and w represent the length and width of the enclosed area, its perimeter is equal to $2l + 2w$; since the fence is positioned x feet from the lot's edges on each side, the perimeter of the lot is $2(l + 2x) + 2(w + 2x)$. Since the amount of money saved by fencing the smaller area is \$432, and since the fencing material costs \$12 per linear foot, 36 fewer feet of material are used to fence around the playground than would have been used to fence around the lot. This can be expressed as the following equation.

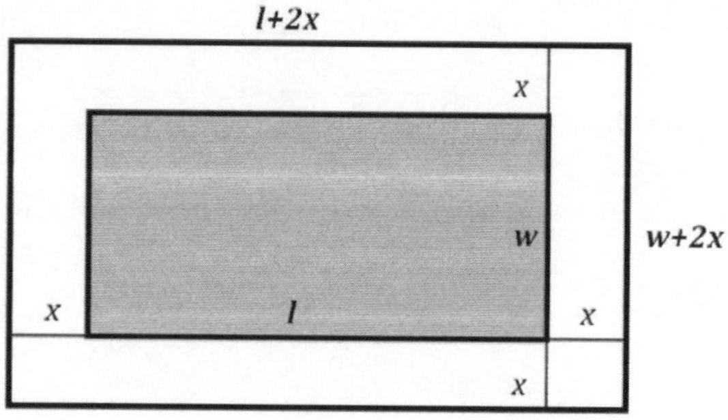

$$2(l + 2x) + 2(w + 2x) - (2l + 2w) = 36$$
$$2l + 4x + 2w + 4x - 2l - 2w = 36$$
$$8x = 36$$
$$x = 4.5 \text{ ft}$$

The difference in the area of the lot and the enclosed space is 141 yd^2, which is the same as 1,269 ft^2. So, $(l + 2x)(w + 2x) - lw = 1{,}269$. Substituting 4.5 for x, we get the following equation that we can solve for $l + w$.

$$(l + 9)(w + 9) - lw = 1{,}269$$
$$lw + 9l + 9w + 81 - lw = 1{,}269$$
$$9l + 9w = 1{,}188$$
$$9(l + w) = 1{,}188$$
$$l + w = 132 \text{ ft}$$

Therefore, the perimeter of the enclosed space, $2(l + w)$, is $2(132) = 264$ ft. The cost of 264 ft of fencing is $264 \times \$12 = \$3{,}168$.

79. C: The line through the center of the box represents the median. The median test score for classes 1 and 2 is 82.

Note that for class 1, the median is a better representation of the data than the mean. There are two low outliers, points which lie outside of two standard deviations from the mean, which bring down the average test score. In cases such as this, the mean is not the best measure of central tendency.

80. B: The problem does not give any information about the size of the bracelet or the spacing between any of the charms. Nevertheless, creating a simple illustration which shows the order of the charms will help when approaching this problem. For example, the circle below represents the bracelet, and the dotted line between A and B represents the clasp. On the right, the line shows the stretched-out bracelet and possible positions of charms C, D, and E based on the parameters.

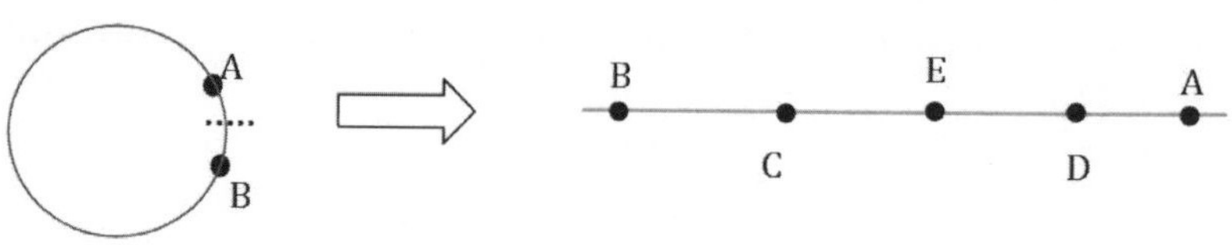

From the drawing above, it appears that statement I is true, but it is not necessarily so. The alternative drawing below also shows the charms ordered correctly, but the distance between B and E is now less than that between D and A.

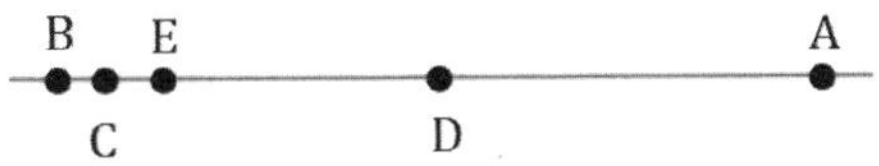

Statement II must be true: charm E must lie between B and D. Statement III must also be true: the distance between charms E and D must be less than that between C and A, which includes charms E and D in the space between them.

81. C: The surface area of a rectangular prism may be calculated using the formula $SA = 2lw + 2wh + 2hl$. Substituting the dimensions of 14 inches, 6 inches, and 8 inches gives $SA = 2(14)(6) + 2(6)(8) + 2(8)(14)$. Thus, the surface area is 488 square inches.

82. D: Let $P(T)$ represent the probability of getting tails on the coin toss. We can see that $P(T) = \frac{1}{2}$. Let $P(P)$ be the chance of getting a prime number on the die. Of the possible outcomes (1 through 6), three are prime (2, 3, and 5), so $P(P) = \frac{3}{6} = \frac{1}{2}$.

Since $P(P)$ and $P(T)$ are not mutually exclusive, $P(P \text{ or } T) = P(P) + P(T) - P(P \text{ and } T)$. Because the events are independent, $P(P \text{ and } T) = P(P) \times P(T)$. Substituting the probability of each event gives $P(P \text{ or } T) = \frac{1}{2} + \frac{1}{2} - \left(\frac{1}{2} \times \frac{1}{2}\right) = \frac{1}{2} + \frac{1}{2} - \frac{1}{4} = \frac{3}{4}$.

83. C: A number that is divisible by 6 is divisible by 2 and 3. A number is divisible by 2 if it is even, and it is divisible by 3 if the sum of the digits is divisible by 3. For example, the number 12 is divisible by 2 and 3, so it is also divisible by 6.

84. A: Marcus needs $325 for the new gaming system. If he earns $6.50 an hour, the number of hours he needs to work can be determined by dividing $325 by $6.50 which is written as $\frac{325}{6.50} = x$. Multiplying both sides of the equation by 6.50 yields $6.50x = 325$.

85. D: In the Dred Scott decision of 1857, the Court ruled that no slave or descendant of slaves could ever be a United States citizen. It also declared the Missouri Compromise of 1820 to be unconstitutional, clearing the way for the expansion of slavery in new American territories. This ruling pleased Southerners and outraged the North, further dividing the nation and setting the stage for war.

86. C: Lying at a little more than 23° south of the equator, the Tropic of Capricorn is the border between the Southern Temperate Zone to the south and the Tropical Zone to the north. The southern hemisphere is tilted toward the sun to its maximum extent each year at the winter solstice in December. The northernmost latitude at which the sun can appear directly overhead is at the Tropic of Cancer during the summer solstice. The northern and southern hemispheres are separated by the equator at 0° latitude. The eastern and western hemispheres are separated by the prime meridian at 0° longitude.

87. B: The Seven Years' War was a global military conflict. In the Americas, the conflict was largely between Western European countries, particularly Great Britain and France.

88. A: The inaccurate statement is the Puritans unconditionally supported the English Reformation. While they agreed with the Reformation in principle, they felt that it had not pursued those principles far enough and should make greater reforms. Similarly, they felt that the Church of England (or Anglican Church), though it had separated from the Catholic Church in the Protestant Reformation, still allowed many practices they found too much like Catholicism. The Puritans did become a chief political power in England because of the first English Civil War between Royalists and Parliamentarians. The Royalists had a profound suspicion of the radical Puritans. Among the Parliament's elements of resistance, the strongest was that of the Puritans. They joined in the battle initially for ostensibly political reasons as others had, but soon they brought more attention to religious issues. Following the Restoration in 1660 and the Uniformity Act of 1662, thereby restoring the Church of England to its pre-English Civil War status, the great majority of Puritan clergy defected from the Church of England. It is also accurate that the Puritans in England disagreed about separating from the Church of England. Some Puritans desired complete separation; they were known first as Separatists and after the Restoration as Dissenters. Others did not want complete separation but instead desired further reform in the Church of England. While they remained part of the Church of England, they were called Non-Separating Puritans, and after the Restoration, they were called Nonconformists.

89. A: The eye wall of a hurricane has the strongest winds and the greatest rainfall. The eye wall is the tower-like rim of the eye. It is from this wall that clouds extend out, which are seen from above as the classic outward spiral pattern. A hurricane front is the outermost edge of its influence; although there will be heavy winds and rain in this area, the intensity will be relatively small. The eye of a hurricane is actually a place of surprising peace. In this area, dry and cool air rushes down to the ground or sea. Once there, the air is caught up in the winds of the eye wall and is driven outward at a furious pace.

90. C: There are no formal qualifications for members of the judicial branch. However, having a background in law is an informal qualification that is considered when appointing Article III judges.

91. C: Paul Revere and William Dawes were both dispatch riders who set out on horseback from Massachusetts to spread news of British troop movements across the American countryside around the beginning of the War of Independence. John Parker was the captain of the Minutemen militia, who were waiting for the British at Lexington, Massachusetts. Samuel Prescott, a young physician, joined Paul Revere and William Dawes along their route.

92. C: Physical geography focuses on processes and patterns in the natural environment. What people eat in any given geographic region is largely dependent on such environmental factors as climate and the availability of arable land. Religion, family, and language may all be affected by geographical factors, but they are not as immediately affected as dietary preferences.

93. A: The phenomenon of "sticky prices" refers to prices that stay the same even though it seems they should change (either increasing or decreasing).

94. A: The 10th Amendment establishes that any power not given to the federal government in the Constitution belongs to the states or the people. The federal and local governments share many responsibilities.

95. C: The Mason-Dixon Line was the manifestation of a border dispute between the British colonies of Pennsylvania, Maryland, and Delaware. It effectively separated, or illustrated, a cultural divide between North and South before the Civil War.

96. A: The Age of Enlightenment was a time of scientific and philosophical achievement. Also called the Age of Reason, it was a time when human thought and reason were prized.

97. A: Rivers promoted the development of the ancient river valley civilizations of the world, including in the Middle East, India, and China. Rivers not only supply water for drinking and crop irrigation, but also provide fertile soil, vegetation for shade cover, food, building materials, and animal life. They additionally allow water travel to other locations. Although some peoples have settled and lived in deserts, they are among the most inhospitable climates. Forests also provide plenty of flora and fauna and exist in areas receiving enough rainfall, but rivers have been historically superior in attracting human societies. Mountains near living areas provide protective barriers; however, though some peoples live there, as in deserts, living in the mountains is difficult due to high altitudes, harsh climates, poor soil for planting, and rough terrain.

98. B: Discretionary spending is dedicated to transportation, education, national resources, the environment, and international affairs. State and local governments use this money to help finance programs. Mandatory spending covers entitlements such as Medicare, Social Security, Federal Retirement, and Medicaid.

99. C: Thomas Jefferson embraced John Locke's concept of separation of church and state. Deism posits that a Supernatural force created the world and universe, but that He did not intervene after creation. Jefferson wanted minimal central governing, just as he viewed the Creator's relationship with the universe.

100. A: Checks and balances were established to keep one branch of government from taking too much authority. When Johnson violated the Tenure of Office Act by replacing Secretary of War Edwin Stanton, Johnson was impeached, but the final vote in the Senate trial came up one vote short of the number needed to convict him.

101. D: The Bill of Rights was drafted by Congress to limit the authority of the government and protect the rights of individual citizens from abuse by the federal government. It was the first document to detail the rights of private citizens.

102. C: If a country's currency increases in value, foreigners will have to give up more of their own currency to get the original country's currency in order to buy the original country's goods and services. This will cause a drop in exports. At the same time, it will be less expensive for people in the original country to exchange their currency for foreign currencies, causing the price of imported goods to drop and the total value of imports to rise.

103. B: There was not a reduction in military spending after the war. Although the manufacturing demand for war supplies and the size of the military decreased, the government had increased military spending from $10 billion in 1947 to more than $50 billion by 1953—a more than fivefold increase. This increase strengthened the American economy. Other factors contributing to the strengthened economy included the significantly higher birth rates during the Baby Boom from 1946 to 1957, which stimulated the growth of the building and automotive industries by increased demand. Government programs, such as the GI Bill (the Servicemen's Readjustment Act of 1944), other veterans' benefits, and the National Defense Education Act all encouraged college enrollments, which increased by nearly four times. Additionally, larger families, increased mobility and low-interest loans offered to veterans led to suburban development and growth as well as increased home construction. Improvements in public health were also results of the new affluence; the rate of infant deaths decreased significantly, and as a result, from 1946–1957, the American life span rose from 67 to 71 years. Moreover, Dr. Jonas Salk developed the polio vaccine in 1955, which virtually wiped out poliomyelitis, preventing many deaths and disabilities in children.

104. C: The Civil Rights Act of 1964 affected the Jim Crow laws in the Southern states. Many minorities suffered under unfair voting laws and segregation. President Lyndon Johnson signed the Civil Rights Act of 1964 into law after the 1963 assassination of President Kennedy, who championed the reform.

105. D: Judaism has existed since around 1300 BC according to historians' estimates. The Greek religion of Stoicism was founded by Zeno in Athens around 313 BC, almost 1,000 years later than Judaism. Confucianism was founded in China by Confucius, who lived from 551 to 479 BC, around 800 years after Judaism. Christianity dates to approximately 30 AD in Israel.

106. D: A market failure is any situation in which the production of a good or service is not efficient. In the cases listed, non-competitive markets allow for the underpayment of labor and the underproduction of a good or service; externalities are negative consequences assumed by parties not involved in a transaction; and public goods are an example of a good the market will not produce at all, or at efficient levels.

107. C: The Druids were neither ignored nor tolerated by the Romans. Conversely, the Druids were viewed as "non-Roman" and therefore were suppressed. Augustus (63 BC–14 AD) forbade Romans to practice Druid rites. According to Pliny, the Senate under Tiberius (42 BC–37 AD) issued a decree suppressing Druids, and in 54 AD, Claudius outlawed Druid rites entirely. It is correct that the Romans generally protected the Jews up until the rebellion in Judea in 66 AD. In fact, Julius Caesar circumvented the Roman laws against "secret societies" by designating Jewish synagogues as "colleges," which in essence permitted Jews to have freedom of worship. After the rebellion in Judea, according to Suetonius, the Emperor Claudius appeared to have expelled all Jews, probably including early Christians, from Rome. The Roman Empire viewed Christianity as a Jewish sect, which was how Christianity began, for 200 years following its emergence. It is also correct that according to Tacitus, when much of the public saw the Emperor Nero as responsible for the Great Fire of Rome in 64 AD, Nero blamed the Christians for the fire in order to deflect guilt from himself. Following their persecution of Jews, the Roman Empire would continue to persecute Christians for the next two centuries.

108. A: Along with stock market speculation, a major cause of the Great Depression was an increased supply of cars, radios, and other goods that was not matched by consumer demand. Industrial production far exceeded the population's purchasing power. Farmers were plagued by overproduction and falling prices while international trade suffered from rising tariffs.

109. B: The President may veto legislation passed by Congress. The executive branch has this "check" on the legislative branch.

110. D: The cinder cone volcano is the most common type of volcano on Earth. A cinder cone has steep sides made of fallen cinders, which themselves are made of the lava that intermittently shoots into the air. A composite volcano, sometimes called the stratovolcano, has steep sides, so the explosions of ash, pumice, and silica are often accompanied by treacherous mudslides. Indeed, it is these mudslides that cause most of the damage associated with composite volcano eruptions. Krakatoa and Mount Saint Helens are examples of composite volcanoes. A lava dome is a round volcano that emits thick lava very slowly. A shield volcano, one example of which is Mt. Kilauea in Hawaii, emits a small amount of lava over an extended period of time. Shield volcanoes are not known for violent eruptions.

111. B: The only true statement is the March on Versailles was made primarily by women. Therefore, an equal number of both men and women did not undertake the March on Versailles.

The women took action because of the dire economic conditions from which they suffered, especially the high prices on bread and food shortages. The storming of the Bastille occurred on July 14, 1789; the March on Versailles occurred on October 5, 1789, almost three months later, not prior to it. (The date of July 14th is so famous as Bastille Day in France that generally it is familiar in other countries as well.) It is not true that the March on Versailles was not effective in accomplishing its purpose. In fact, the marchers did achieve their goal: They stormed the palace and killed several guards. La Fayette, in charge of the National Guard to control the mob, convinced the royals to move from Versailles to Paris and to stop blocking the National Assembly, and the royal family complied with these demands. The women did not march right to Versailles with no preliminaries. First, they assembled in markets around Paris and marched to the Hôtel de Ville. There they made their demands of the Paris city officials. When those officials did not give acceptable responses, the women then joined a march to the palace at Versailles. While the march to Versailles included men and weapons, some 7,000 women made up the majority of the marchers.

112. D: America is a common law country because English common law was adopted in all states except Louisiana. Common law is based on precedent and changes over time. Each state develops its own common laws.

113. C: George Washington served 2 four-year terms as president. This interval of time was not specified in the Constitution, but future presidents followed suit (until FDR).

114. A: Animals of the phylum Mollusca or mollusks, respire (breathe) through gills. Respiration is the process of taking in oxygen and releasing carbon dioxide. Mollusca consists of several classes that include species as diverse as chitons, clams, land and marine snails, and squid. This represents a diverse range of body structures. Many mollusks have a mantle that includes a cavity that is used for both breathing and excretion. Within the mantle are gills (ctenidia). Mollusks do not have tracheas. Some land snails have a respiratory cavity that is often called a lung but is not a true lung. Spiders, which are not mollusks (they are arachnids), have a type of lungs called book lungs. Muscle contraction is not required for the gills to function. Other structures, such as cilia, work to pass water over the gills.

115. D: The equation for power, $power = \frac{work}{time}$, can be utilized. The mass of the object (10 kg) and the distance (10 m) can be used to calculate work, $work = mass \times (gravitational\ acceleration) \times distance$. The value for time is provided.

116. B: Gradualism states that evolution occurs slowly, with organisms exhibiting small changes over long periods of time. According to gradualism, the fossil record should show gradual changes over time. Punctuated equilibrium states that evolution occurs in spurts of sudden change. According to punctuated equilibrium, the fossil record should have large gaps.

117. D: Igneous rocks are formed when magma in the Earth erupts through cracks in the crust. There, the lava cools, creating a hard structure with many air pockets or holes.

118. A: In the food chain of tree → caterpillar → frog → snake → hawk → worm, the tree is at the trophic level with the greatest amount of energy. Trophic level refers to the position of an organism in a food chain. Energy is lost according to the laws of thermodynamics as one moves up the food chain because it is converted to heat when consumers consume. Primary producers, such as autotrophs, are organisms who are at the base and capture solar energy. Primary consumers are herbivores that feed on the producers. Secondary consumers consume primary consumers and so on. Decomposers get their energy from the consumption of dead plants and animals.

119. B: Temperature is a measure of the kinetic energy of particles. As temperature increases, the average kinetic energy also increases. As the gas particles move more rapidly, they occupy a larger volume. The increase in speed of the individual particles combined with the greater distance over which any intermolecular forces must act results in a decrease in the intermolecular forces.

120. B: An apple turning brown is an example of a chemical change; in this case, oxidation. During a chemical change, one substance is changed into another. Sublimation of water refers to the conversion between the solid and the gaseous phases of matter, with no intermediate liquid stage. This is a phase change, not a chemical reaction. Dissolution of salt in water refers to a physical change since the salt and water can be separated again by evaporating the water. Pulverized rock is an example of a physical change where the form has changed but not the substance itself.

121. C: Covalent compounds are usually formed by the combination of two or more non-metallic elements with one another. In these compounds, atoms share electrons. Ionic compounds are most often formed between a metal and a nonmetal. Organic compounds are covalent compounds that contain carbon and hydrogen atoms. Some of the compounds formed by non-metallic elements are polar, but not all of them.

122. C: Vinegar fizzing when poured on a rock is an example of chemical weathering. Mechanical and chemical weathering are processes that break down rocks. Mechanical weathering breaks down rocks physically but does not change their chemical composition. Frost and abrasion are examples. Water, oxygen, carbon dioxide, and living organisms can lead to the chemical weathering of rock. Vinegar is a weak acid and will undergo a chemical reaction, evidenced by fizzing, with the rock. Choice A, rain freezing on the roadway, is an example of the phase change of water from a liquid to a solid and may lead to physical weathering. Choice B, ivy growing on the side of a wooden house, is incorrect since the house is not a rock. Choice D, a river carrying sediment downstream, is an example of erosion.

123. A: Descriptive studies look at and analyze the characteristics of a population or compare aspects across multiple populations. These studies seek information about the state of a population as it is rather than experimentally investigating cause-and-effect relationships by manipulating variables and observing outcomes. Comparing the heights of male and female penguins is an example of a descriptive study. The subject is strictly an observable measure (height) of established populations (male and female). For the other studies, the focus is on the cause-and-effect relationship between a manipulated variable (different media, drug vs. placebo, and old vs. new descriptions) and a result of interest (growth rate, drug efficacy, sales).

124. D: The temperature of a substance during the time of any phase change remains the same. In this case, the phase change was from liquid to solid, or freezing. Latent heat of fusion, in this case, is energy that is released from the substance as it reforms its solid form. This energy will be released and the liquid will turn to solid before the temperature of the substance will decrease further. If the substance were changing from solid to liquid, the heat of fusion would be the amount of heat required to break apart the attractions between the molecules in the solid form to change to the liquid form. The latent heat of fusion is exactly the same quantity of energy for a substance for either melting or freezing. Depending on the process, this amount of heat would either be absorbed by the substance (melting) or released (freezing).

125. D: Chemical equations must be balanced on each side of the reaction. Balancing means the total number of atoms stays the same, but their arrangement within specific reactants and products can change. The law of conservation of matter states that matter can never be created or destroyed.

Heat may be absorbed or released in a reaction; these are classified as endothermic and exothermic reactions, respectively. The rate of the reaction increases with temperature for most reactions.

126. C: Fossils are least likely to be found in igneous rock. Igneous rock is formed by extreme heat as magma escapes through the Earth's crust and cools. The remains of plants and animals in fossil form are not usually preserved under these conditions. Sedimentary rock (A) is where most fossils are found. Sedimentary rock is formed more slowly and is very abundant. Since soft mud and silts compress into layers, organisms can also be deposited. Metamorphic rock (B) is rock that has undergone change by heat and pressure. This usually destroys any fossils, but occasionally fossil remains are simply distorted and can be found in metamorphic rock.

127. B: It is true that rocks are classified by their formation and the minerals they contain, while minerals are classified by their chemical composition and physical properties. Choice A is incorrect because rocks may contain traces of organic compounds. Choices C and D are incorrect because only minerals can be polymorphs and only rocks contain mineraloids.

128. D: Isotopes are variations of an element that have different numbers of neutrons. The various isotopes of an element have the same numbers of protons and electrons. For example, carbon has three naturally occurring isotopes: carbon-12, carbon-13 and carbon-14 (which is radioactive). Isotopes of an element differ in mass number, which is the number of protons and neutrons added together, but have the same atomic number, or number of protons.

129. B: If a gas and a liquid are placed in a sealed container, cooling the liquid will help dissolve the gas into the liquid. Gases have higher solubility in liquids at lower temperatures. At higher temperatures, the gas molecules will have more kinetic energy and will have enough energy to overcome intermolecular interactions with the liquid solvent and leave the solution. This also explains why heating the liquid is incorrect. Shaking the container is also incorrect as this would give the gas energy to escape. Decreasing the pressure on the lid may or may not significantly affect the pressure inside the vessel depending on the nature of the vessel, but decreasing the pressure inside the vessel would decrease the solubility of the gas in the liquid.

130. B: The freezing point of sea water is lower than that of fresh water as sea water is denser. It is denser because it has more dissolved salts. The freezing point changes with salinity, pressure, and density, but can be as low as –2 °C (28.4 °F), compared with 0 °C (32 °F) for fresh water.

131. C: Tropical climate zones are characterized by frequent rainfall, especially during the monsoon season, and by moderate temperatures that vary little from season to season or between night and day. Tropical zones do experience frequent rainfall, which leads to abundant vegetation.

132. D: The process whereby a radioactive element releases energy slowly over a long period of time to lower its energy and become more stable is best described as decay. The nucleus undergoing decay, known as the parent nuclide, spontaneously releases energy most commonly through the emission of an alpha particle, a beta particle, or a gamma ray. The changed nucleus, called the daughter nuclide, is now more stable than the parent nuclide, although the daughter nuclide may undergo another decay to an even more stable nucleus. A decay chain is a series of decays of a radioactive element into different elements.

133. A: A lysosome is an organelle that is thought to be linked to the aging process and contains digestive enzymes that break down food and unneeded substances. Chromatin is the structure created by DNA and various proteins in the cell's nucleus during interphase and condenses to form chromosomes. Plastids are found in plants and algae. They often contain pigments and usually help make chemical compounds for the plant. The Golgi apparatus prepares macromolecules like proteins and lipids for transport.

134. C: On a topographic map, an area where the contour lines are very close together indicates that the slope is very steep. Lines very far apart would indicate a more gradual change in elevation. Contour lines help represent the actual shape of the Earth's surface features and geographic landmarks like rivers, lakes, and vegetation. Topographic maps also show man-made features such as roads, dams, and major buildings. They are based on aerial photography, and the quadrangle maps are produced in various scales. The 7.5-minute quadrangle is very common and provides a 1:24,000 scale, where 1 inch represents 2,000 feet.

135. A: The average distance from the earth to the sun is equal to one astronomical unit (AU). An AU is equal to 93 million miles and is far smaller than a light-year or a parsec. A light-year is defined as the distance light can travel in a vacuum in one year, and is equal to roughly 63,241 AU. A parsec is the parallax of one arcsecond and is equal to 2.0626×10^5 astronomical units.

136. D: Sound cannot travel through a vacuum, though it doesn't necessarily suggest that it *can* travel through solids. Nor does the fact that atoms are packed tightly together demonstrate the fact that sound can travel through a solid. The fact that a sound is produced by knocking on a solid object also does not prove sound can pass through the object. However, if you hear a sound on the other side of a solid wall, the sound must have traveled through the wall.

137. A: Anthophyta is a division of plants that produces seeds as part of reproduction. Spermatopyta is the broader group that includes all plants that produce seeds for reproduction, which includes gymnosperms and angiosperms (the same group as anthophyta). Anthophyta are also known as the group that contains flowering plants. It is the largest and most diverse grouping of plants and includes many food, clothing, and medicinal uses for humans. Grains, beans, nuts, fruits, vegetables, spices, tea, coffee, chocolate, cotton, linen, and aspirin are all derived from plants from anthophyta. Lycophyta is a small group of plants including club mosses and scale trees. Sphenophyta contains about thirty species including horsetails, foxtails, or scouring rushes. Pterophyta contains non-seed plants like ferns. Lycophyta, sphenophyta, and pterophyta all use spores to reproduce sexually.

138. A: A magnetic field is created by a spin magnetic dipole moment and the orbital magnetic dipole moment of the electrons in atoms. Therefore, it is the spinning and rotating of electrons in atoms that creates a magnetic field. The separation of charged particles in atoms describes the nucleus and electron clouds within an atom. The vibrational and translational motion of atoms creates thermal energy. Loosely held valence electrons surrounding an atom indicates a good electrical conductor.

139. D: The asteroid belt in our solar system is located between Mars and Jupiter. The asteroid belt is populated by asteroids and dwarf planets that are distributed thinly enough that spacecraft can pass through the belt with relative ease.

140. D: In a parallel circuit, the voltage is the same for all three paths. Because the resistance is different on each path but the voltage is the same, Ohm's law dictates that the current will also be different for each path. Ohm's law says that current is inversely related to resistance. Therefore, the current will be greatest in path C as it has the least resistance, 2 ohms.

141. D: Lower seed dispersal is not an advantage that angiosperms show over other types of plants. Gymnosperms, for example, have plentiful amounts of pollen, but it does not always hit its mark. Angiosperms are the most recently evolved plant division and contain at least 260,000 extant species. They are very diverse and occupy many habitats. Many other species in other plant divisions do not have true leaves. Gymnosperms have modified leaves in the form of needles. Double fertilization refers to how one sperm cell fuses with an ovule, forming the zygote. The second sperm forms into a triploid endosperm that provides energy for the embryo.

142. A: Visual literacy can best be described as the ability to communicate through images and comprehend the messages contained in images. In visual literacy education, students are taught not only to create images that appropriately communicate information, but also to interpret and derive meaning from both artistic and informational images.

143. C: Allegro is a tempo that ranges between 120 and 168 beats per minute (bpm). While allegro can be thought of as a "quick" tempo, it is not as fast as presto, played between 168 and 200 bpm. Therefore, (A) is incorrect. Moderato and largo—played between 108-120 and 40-60, respectively—are slower tempos, proving (B) and (D) incorrect.

144. B: A fresco is actually a painting style that involves applying paint or pigment directly to plaster. In order to give pigment the desired consistency for fluid painting, several things can be mixed with the pigment: egg tempera; water; turpentine, which is used as a cleaner and thinner; or oil, which has the opposite effect to turpentine, making the paint thicker.

145. A: The threads that are stretched taut across the loom before weaving begins are called the warp. The weft threads are the threads that are woven across the warp, and the loom is the apparatus used for weaving. Twill is a weaving technique that produces a weave with parallel, diagonal lines.

146. A: Multiple research studies repeatedly demonstrate that cardiovascular diseases, diabetes, and colon and breast cancer risks are lowered by regular physical activity (PA). Researchers recommend 30 to 60 minutes a day of PA to reduce the risks of breast and colon cancer significantly, and 150 minutes a week to decrease risks of cardiovascular diseases and diabetes. Thirty minutes a day for five days a week equals 150 minutes a week; therefore, the amounts needed are similar to lower the risks of these diseases. (Sixty minutes is double this and may afford some people greater cancer risk reduction.) Hence, risks for all these diseases are lowered, not some. The amounts necessary to reduce risk do not vary greatly among these diseases. Regular PA in adequate amounts does lower disease risk.

147. D: Johannes Brahms composed music in the middle to late 19th century. Therefore, Brahms is most strongly associated with the Romantic Period in classical music, which ran from about 1815 to about 1910. Bach is most strongly associated with the Baroque Period (1600-1760), and Ravel is most closely associated with the Impressionist Period (1890-1940). Aaron Copland, often is considered "the dean of American composers" and composed music in the mid to late 20th century; he would not fit into any of the above listed periods.

148. B: Form is an artistic element that would only apply to three-dimensional art forms, such as sculptures or decorative arts. Two-dimensional works of art have the element of shape, which refers to their length and width, while three-dimensional works of art have the element of form, which refers to their length, width, and depth. Proportion and balance are both *principles* of art that would apply to both two- and three-dimensional works. Line is an artistic element that would be applicable to both types of art.

149. C: By correctly rendering proportion in her work, an artist can achieve a sense of realism. Correctly rendering proportion involves depicting the size relationships within and among objects as they are actually perceived by the human eye. For example, objects in the foreground of a painting should generally be larger than objects in the background (even if they are smaller in real life) since this is how the human eye perceives them.

150. A: Artists will often use portfolios to demonstrate their capabilities. Portfolios are not designed to communicate past work history or education and are rarely used for teaching purposes. The intention of a portfolio is not to showcase an artist's entire body of work, but instead to highlight select pieces. A portfolio is also not intended to lay claim to copyright privileges.

Practice Test #2

Refer to the following for question 1:

Ms. Baird assigns students a historical fiction short story to read. She wants to check her students' individual comprehension skills, specifically their ability to support an idea with evidence from the text. However, one student appears to be struggling with the story. Ms. Baird gives this student a graphic organizer containing the following sentence stems: *Someone, Wanted, But, So, Then.*

1. Which scenario is the best way to accomplish Ms. Baird's goals of assessing individual comprehension skills?

a. Split the students into groups after reading the text as a class and allow them to work together on a worksheet activity she has designed.
b. Play a game in which Ms. Baird posts a card with a main idea. Students read silently and independently and raise their hands to answer when they have found a transition in the plot.
c. As a class, brainstorm main ideas, topics, or concepts from a text. Allow students to choose a select number of these ideas and copy them onto separate index cards. The students then should individually review the text, recording any supporting evidence on the notecard with the applicable main idea.
d. Administer a comprehension quiz during class. Allow students to switch papers and grade each other's work. Next, students can spend the remainder of the class period discussing the answers so that each one understands the text fully.

2. Another name for a persuasive essay is:

a. Dynamic essay
b. Convincing essay
c. Argumentative essay
d. Position paper

3. The teacher and her students brainstorm a list of talents, skills, and specialized knowledge belonging to members of the class. Some of the items on the list include how to make a soufflé, how to juggle, and how to teach a dog to do tricks. One student knows a great deal about spiders, and another knows about motorcycles. The teacher asks the students to each write an essay about something they are good at or know a great deal about. What kind of essay is she asking the students to produce?

a. Cause and effect
b. Compare/contrast
c. Expository
d. Argumentative

4. What is the primary reason the early 21st century has been referred to as the Information Age?

a. Most organizations need more information than ever before.
b. There are more sources and outputs of information than ever before.
c. Privacy and the protection of information are more important than ever before.
d. People are seeking more information about a wider variety of topics than ever before.

5. Which choice constitutes the best method for building conceptual vocabulary?

a. Using word webs to organize thinking about related terms
b. Previewing vocabulary words for upcoming units in other subjects such as science or social studies
c. Implementing a framework for introducing students to various concepts over time
d. Practicing sight words

6. A third-grade teacher has several students reading above grade level. Most of the remaining students are reading at grade level. There are also a few students reading below grade level. She decides to experiment. Her hypothesis is that by giving the entire class a chapter book above grade level, high-level readers will be satisfied, grade-level readers will be challenged in a positive way, and students reading below grade level will be inspired to improve. Her method is most likely to:

a. Succeed, producing students reading at an Instructional reading level. High-level readers will be happy to be given material appropriate to their reading level. Grade-level readers will challenge themselves to improve reading strategies in order to master the text. Because only a few of the students are reading below grade level, the other students, who feel happy and energized, will inspire the slower readers by modeling success.
b. Succeed, producing students reading at an Independent reading level. High-level readers will independently help grade-level readers who will, in turn, independently help those below grade level.
c. Fail, producing students at a Frustration reading level. Those reading below grade level are likely to give up entirely. Those reading at grade level are likely to get frustrated and form habits that will actually slow down their development.
d. Fail, producing students reading at a Chaotic reading level. By nature, children are highly competitive. The teacher has not taken into consideration multiple learning styles. The children who are at grade level will either become bitter and angry at those whose reading level is above grade level or simply give up. The children reading below grade level will not be able to keep up and will in all likelihood act out their frustration or completely shut down.

7. A teacher is working with a group of English language learners. She asks them to take two pieces of paper. At the top of the first paper, they are to write *SAME*, and at the top of the other, *DIFFERENT*. Each child will consider what his native country and the United States have in common, and what distinct features each country possesses. The children are using which method in organizing their ideas?

a. Hunt and peck
b. Consider and persuade
c. Evaluate and contrast
d. Compare and contrast

8. Which of the following reflects MLA guidelines for citing internet sources with regard to page numbers in in-text citations in research papers?

a. A source from the internet should not be used if it does not include page numbers in any form.
b. If a printout from a website has page numbers, citations should include these numbers.
c. In-text citations of online sources in research papers should never include page numbers.
d. If the source is a PDF file, the page numbers from the file should be in citations.

9. English language learner (ELL) students typically are able to develop which type of English language skills the fastest?

a. They typically develop BICS much sooner than CALP.
b. They typically develop CALP more quickly than BICS.
c. They typically develop both at about the same rates.
d. They develop these at individually varying speeds.

Refer to the following for question 10:

A third-grade science teacher gives her students one hour to read an article about penguins, take notes on important information, and use the notes to write a three-paragraph expository essay. Before they begin, the teacher writes the words *Spheniscidae*, *plumage*, and *Aptenodytes forsteri* on the board. She explains the meaning of each word. At the end of the hour, one student, Joshua, only has his notes completed. The teacher examines his notes, part of which are shown below.

> Penguins are animals that live in the Southern Hemisphere.
> Many people believe that penguins live in the Arctic, but that is not true.
> Penguins in Antarctica huddle together to stay warm. They take turns standing on the outside of the huddle, where it is colder.
> Penguins' feathers help protect them from the water and cold air.
> Penguins live in groups called colonies.

10. The words written by the teacher on the board are examples of:

a. Academic words
b. Alliteration
c. Content-specific words
d. Ionization

11. The phrase "pretty as a picture" is best described as a:

a. Metaphor
b. Simile
c. Synecdoche
d. Paradox

12. Which of the following statements is most accurate about writing the introduction of an essay?

a. The introduction should move from the broad and general to the focused and specific.
b. The introduction should save the most attention-getting material for later in the work.
c. The introduction should move from the focused and specific to the broad and general.
d. The introduction should use the technique of starting essays with dictionary definitions.

13. A school has a policy of only permitting administration of its first choice among standardized formal assessments of phonological development twice per school year to conserve money and time. A first-grade teacher wanting to inform her instructional planning, implementation, and adjustments appropriately can do which of these?

a. Stick to the school's policy and do the best she can with the results
b. Lobby administrators to change policy to giving this test more often
c. Use informal assessments continually and exclusively
d. Conduct informal and other formal assessments on an ongoing basis

14. Phonemic awareness is a type of:

a. Phonological awareness. Phonemic awareness is the ability to recognize sounds within words.
b. Phonics. It is a teaching technique whereby readers learn the relationship between letters and sounds.
c. Alphabetization. Unless a reader knows the alphabet, phonemic awareness is useless.
d. Syntactical awareness. Understanding the underlying structure of a sentence is key to understanding meaning.

15. What is the purpose of targeted instruction?

a. Deliver instructions that are precise, clear, and direct so that students understand exactly what is expected.
b. Accurately rank a group of learners from low achievers to high achievers so that the teacher knows from the beginning of the school year which students have less ability and will therefore need support.
c. Teach students how to take information from a text and reorganize it into bulleted lists.
d. Assess and target areas needing improvement as well as areas of greatest strength for each student to ensure that all members of a class are receiving instruction tailored to their specific needs.

16. Which choice most appropriately fills the blanks in this statement? "In writing, _____ is the writer's attitude as evident from the writing, and _____ is the individual way in which the writer expresses themselves through the writing."

a. voice, tone
b. tone, voice
c. style, tone
d. voice, style

17. Which of the following literary elements are most likely to be found in both fictional narratives and nonfictional informational text?

a. The writing style of the author
b. Labeled diagrams and photos
c. Excitement and drama
d. Themes and plots

18. *Train, brain, spring.* The underlined letters are examples of:

a. Consonant digraph
b. Consonant blend
c. Consonant shift
d. Continental shift

19. A student is taking a reading test. The teacher has blocked out a number of words. Each blank is assigned a set of three possible words. The student must select the correct word from each set so that the text makes sense. The student is taking:

a. A cloze test
b. A maze test
c. A multiple-choice quiz
d. A vocabulary test

20. A writing assignment asks the student to do things like organize, plan, formulate, assemble, compose, construct, or arrange some material they have read or learned. Which of the following cognitive (learning) objectives is the teacher aiming to meet with this assignment?

a. Analysis
b. Synthesis
c. Evaluation
d. Application

21. Following a typical developmental sequence, which of the following is expected of second graders in decoding and identifying new or unfamiliar words?

a. Identifying new words and compound words via phonics, roots, suffixes, and analogies
b. Identifying new word meanings through knowledge of familiar synonyms and antonyms
c. Identifying new word meanings by comparing to known homophones and homographs
d. Identifying new word meanings by roots, prefixes, suffixes, idioms, and dictionary markings

22. "Decoding" is also called:

a. Remediation
b. Deciphering
c. Alphabetic principle
d. Deconstruction

23. A teacher has given her students an assignment to write a non-rhyming poem of three lines. The first and last lines each contain five syllables, and the middle line contains seven syllables. The students are writing a:

a. Limerick
b. Metaphor
c. Villanelle
d. Haiku

24. Which of the following would be most useful in assessing and documenting students' language progress throughout a school year?

a. An audio/video recording of each student reading the same text at the beginning of the year and again at the end of the year
b. A portfolio including pre-tests, post-tests, vocabulary work, journal entries, writing assignments, group projects, and other relevant work from throughout the year
c. Score composites and details from state- and national-referenced exams or other standardized tests.
d. A detailed narrative composed by the student's teacher, detailing strengths, weaknesses, and descriptions of the student's work.

25. Of the following statements, which is true about the relationship of reading fluency, word decoding, and reading comprehension?

a. Developing fluency in reading has no relationship to speed and automaticity with decoding words.
b. Students should have strong word recognition foundations established before fluency instruction.
c. Reading fluency shows faster information processing speed, but has no impact on comprehension.
d. Slower, less automatic word decoding decreases reading fluency, but it increases comprehension.

26. A reading teacher is assessing an eighth grader to determine her reading level. Timed at a minute, the student reads with 93% accuracy. She misreads an average of seven words out of 100. What is her reading level?

a. She is reading at a Frustration level.
b. She is reading at a Listening level.
c. She is reading at an Instructional level.
d. She is reading at an Independent level.

27. Which of the following aspects of poetic form is characteristic of haiku?

a. A 5-7-5 syllable pattern
b. An ABA rhyme scheme
c. Perfectly regular meter
d. Lengthy epic narratives

28. Which of the following statements is most true?

a. Introducing oral and written texts from a variety of cultures can enhance students' understanding and appreciation of language.
b. Children typically learn language best when exposed primarily to texts exemplary of their own background or culture, thereby increasing their ability to identify personally with what they are learning.
c. Studying other languages will impair a student's ability to develop his or her own first language.
d. Students should be exposed to one type of text at a time to diminish genre confusion.

29. A teacher writes four sentences on the board and instructs his students to copy the sentences from the board into their notebooks. They must capitalize words with suffixes. Which sentence is correct?

a. The PRINCE declared his undying love for the PRINCESS.
b. Television is a form of MULTIMEDIA.
c. This loud, loud noise is very DISPLEASING.
d. The BOOKKEEPER examined every page of the rare play.

30. Which of the following statements regarding the acquisition of language is FALSE?

a. Young children often have the ability to comprehend written language just as early as they can comprehend or reproduce oral language when given appropriate instruction.
b. Oral language typically develops before a child understands the relationship between spoken and written words.
c. Most young children are first exposed to written language when an adult reads aloud.
d. A child's ability to speak, read, and write depends on a variety of physiological factors, as well as environmental factors.

31. A teacher asks her students to say the word *map*. She then says, "Change the /m/ sound to a /t/ sound. What word do you have now?" Which phonemic awareness skill are students practicing?

a. Alliteration
b. Segmenting
c. Blending onset and rime
d. Phoneme substitution

32. A classroom is comprised of students with varying abilities in language. Some students can read fluently, while others are still just learning. Speech and language abilities also range widely among the students. Which approach best suits this class?

a. Each student begins with reading texts slightly below their ability level and practices reading aloud with partners and teachers to build skills.
b. The teacher consistently presents challenging material for students, knowing that when students are held to high expectations, they typically rise to meet a challenge.
c. The teacher splits the classroom into groups based on ability and appoints a group leader to guide other students.
d. The class is exposed to a variety of "texts," in combination with direct phonetic and vocabulary instruction, including written text, video, song, and spoken stories.

33. To help students understand abstract concepts in the print materials they read, which instructional aids that teachers provide can students always use three-dimensionally?

a. Examples
b. Manipulatives
c. Graphic organizers
d. Charts, tables, and graphs

34. Examples of CVC words include:

a. Add, pad, mad
b. Cat, tack, act
c. Elephant, piano, examine
d. Dog, sit, leg

35. In first-language (L1) and second-language (L2) acquisition, which of the following is true about language acquisition stages?

a. L2 learners do not undergo the first stage, called the "silent period," as L1 learners do.
b. L2 learners undergo all stages, but they are urged to skip the first stage more than L1s.
c. L2 learners do not undergo the second stage, "formulaic speech," as L1 learners do.
d. L2 learners undergo the third stage, "structural and semantic simplifications," later.

36. Which of the following is the best use of technology in a language arts classroom?

a. Providing laptops to students to achieve more effective note-taking, access to word processing programs, and access to the internet
b. Encouraging the use of slide shows or similar programs to support lectures and oral presentations, as well as to organize pertinent class concepts
c. Incorporating a computer-based "language lab" in which students can listen to texts and engage in interactive word-study and comprehension activities
d. Whenever possible, watching film interpretations based on texts studied in class

37. Which of the following is the correct sequence of these phases of spelling development?

a. Semiphonetic, precommunicative, transitional, correct, phonetic
b. Precommunicative, semiphonetic, phonetic, transitional, correct
c. Correct, phonetic, semiphonetic, precommunicative, transitional
d. Phonetic, semiphonetic, transitional, correct, precommunicative

38. Context clues are useful in:

a. Predicting future action
b. Understanding the meaning of words that are not familiar
c. Understanding character motivation
d. Reflecting on a text's theme

39. Which of the following statements is correct regarding Standard English?

a. Standard English does not allow for variations of dialect.
b. Rules from standard English apply to written language.
c. Standard English is universal in English-speaking nations.
d. No standard English exists that is actually used in practice.

40. Which choice is the best method of structuring language arts curriculum and instruction?

a. Examine all state-level or national standardized tests that students will be required to take. Structure the curriculum and lessons to address all concepts included in the tests, with an attempt to proportion the time spent in a way that mirrors the breakdown of the tests.
b. Research the instructional methods used in supplemental education fields. Use those newer methods of introducing and reinforcing concepts in class to ensure that students are receiving consistent and standard instruction.
c. Use the written curriculum provided by the school district or specific campus as a foundation for instruction. Schedule regular planning sessions to incorporate a variety of texts and instruction methods, as well as to coordinate instruction with teachers of other subjects.
d. Plan sequential units of study that focus on isolated skills such as word and vocabulary study, comprehension strategies, listening, viewing, and speaking. Design lessons to focus on the mastery of one skill at a time with the goal of studying the relationship between skills toward the end of the school year.

41. Which of the following is NOT an English Language Arts expectation for middle school students in the English Language Arts subject area?

a. To interpret and understand visual imagery, meanings, and messages
b. To conduct analyses and critiques of how visual media are important
c. To produce visual media representations communicating with others
d. To get ideas from the environment, and develop and organize them

42. Syllable types include:

a. Closed, open, silent *e*, vowel team, vowel-*r*, and consonant-*le*
b. Closed, open, silent, double-vowel, *r*, and *le*
c. Closed, midway, open, emphasized, prefixed, and suffixed
d. Stressed, unstressed, and silent

43. The English language word *noob* is an example of the result of which linguistic process?

a. Blending
b. Conversion
c. Neologisms
d. Onomatopoeia

44. A teacher designs lessons for the upcoming week. During the first part of the week, the teacher is going to divide the class into two sections. While one group is working independently on their projects, the other group will sit in a circle. The teacher has broken a story up into several sections, and each student will read a section aloud. The teacher will note for her records how many errors a student makes. She will also administer a brief verbal "quiz" to which the students will respond in writing. The combination of verbal reading results and comprehension quiz results will give her a better understanding of each child's abilities and/or needs. What kind of assessment did this teacher use?

a. Cloze-style
b. Informal reading inventory
c. Student response form
d. Articulation assessment

45. Among assessments of reading comprehension, which of these compares student scores to the average scores of a sample of students representing the same population?

a. A norm-referenced state test
b. An informal reading inventory
c. A curriculum-based assessment
d. A criterion-referenced state test

46. Word-recognition ability is:

a. Equally important to all readers
b. Used only by fluent readers
c. Another term for "word attack"
d. Especially important to English language learners and students with reading disabilities

47. Which choice describes a primary benefit of an adult reading aloud to a group of elementary students?

a. Students have a chance to rest their minds and enjoy oral language.
b. The adult can model reading fluently for students still building reading skills.
c. Students have time and opportunity to work on individual projects and assignments while listening to the story.
d. The adult transmits a great deal of conceptual knowledge via auditory instruction, which is especially beneficial for students who are auditory learners.

48. A dartboard consists of two concentric circles with radii of 3 inches and 6 inches. If a dart is thrown onto the board, what is the probability the dart will land in the inner circle?

a. $\frac{1}{4}$
b. $\frac{1}{2}$
c. $\frac{1}{3}$
d. $\frac{1}{5}$

49. A ball has a diameter of 7 inches. Which of the following best represents the volume?

a. 165.7 in^3
b. 179.6 in^3
c. 184.5 in^3
d. 192.3 in^3

50. Which of the following pairs of equations represents the lines of symmetry in the figure below?

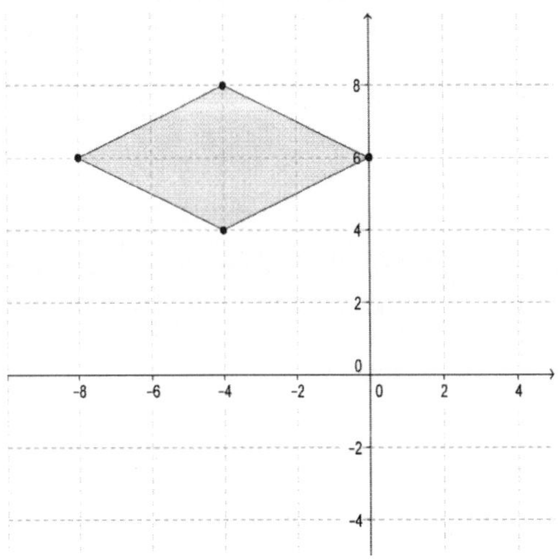

a. $x = -4, y = 6$
b. $x = 4, y = 6$
c. $y = -4, x = 6$
d. $y = 4, x = -6$

51. Which of these graphs is NOT representative of the data set shown below?

3|6799
4|23889
5|0111158
6|00123

Key
2|123 = 21, 22, 23

a. 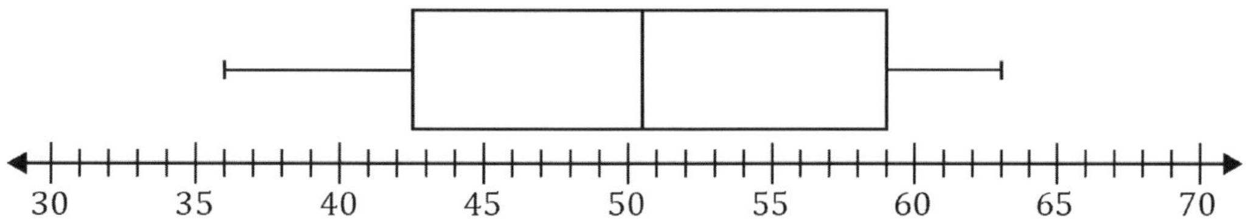

b. 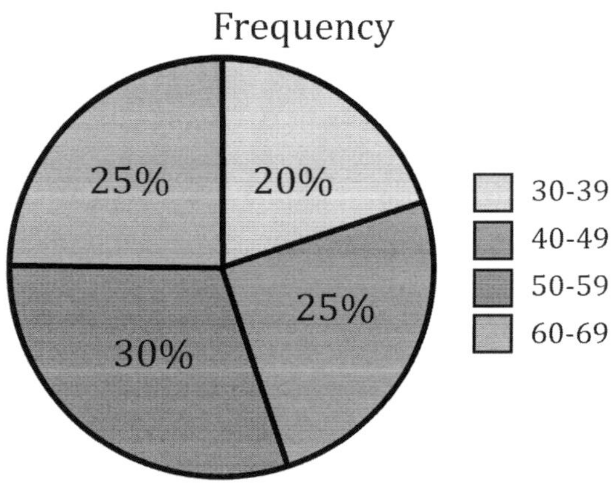

c. 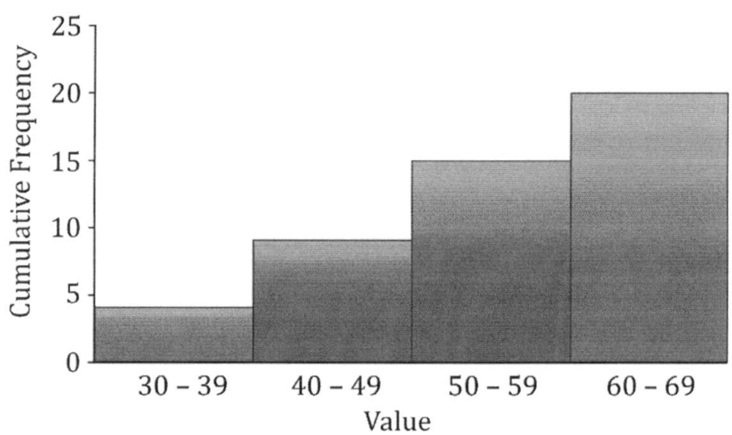

d. All of these graphs represent the data set.

52. Zeke drove from his house to a furniture store in Atlanta and then back home along the same route. It took Zeke three hours to drive to the store. By driving an average of 20 mph faster on his return trip, Zeke was able to save an hour of driving time. What was Zeke's average driving speed on his round trip?

a. 24 mph
b. 48 mph
c. 50 mph
d. 60 mph

53. For which of these does a rotation of 120° about the center of the polygon map the polygon onto itself?

a. Square
b. Regular hexagon
c. Regular octagon
d. Regular decagon

54. Marlon pays $45 for a jacket that has been marked down 25%. What was the original cost of the jacket?

a. $80
b. $75
c. $65
d. $60

55. Aidan has a plastic container in the shape of a square pyramid. He wants to fill the container with chocolate candies. If the base has a side length of 6 inches and the height of the container is 9 inches, how many cubic inches of space may be filled with candies?

a. 98
b. 102
c. 108
d. 112

56. Mr. Sarver, a second-grade teacher, notices that a few of his students are struggling with the concept of borrowing when subtracting two-digit numbers. Which of the following activities would best help students understand this concept of borrowing?

a. The teacher works subtraction problems on the whiteboard.
b. The students watch a children's video about borrowing.
c. The students complete a worksheet with subtraction problems.
d. The students use cardboard manipulatives to model subtraction problems.

57. Coach Weybright's 6th-grade basketball team has played 36 games this season. The ratio of wins to losses is 2 : 1. If x represents the number of wins, which of the following proportions can be used to determine the number of wins?

a. $\frac{x}{36} = \frac{2}{1}$
b. $\frac{x}{2} = \frac{1}{36}$
c. $\frac{x}{3} = \frac{36}{2}$
d. $\frac{x}{36} = \frac{2}{3}$

58. Mr. Orr asks his class to use inductive reasoning to determine the pattern in this sequence of numbers. Which number is next in this series?

2, 5, 10, 17, __

a. 22
b. 24
c. 25
d. 26

59. Given that the two horizontal lines in the diagram below are parallel, which pair of angles is congruent?

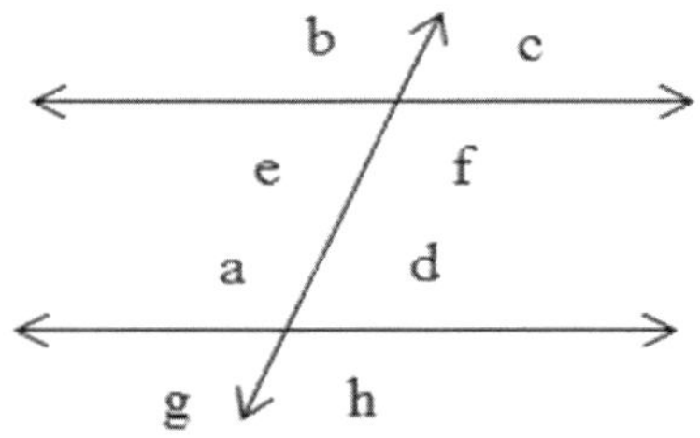

a. ∠e and ∠b
b. ∠d and ∠h
c. ∠g and ∠c
d. ∠d and ∠f

60. Which number comes next in the sequence?

16, 24, 34, 46, 60

a. 56
b. 72
c. 74
d. 76

61. The set $\{a, b, c, d\}$ forms a group under operation #. Which of these statements is (are) true about the group?

#	***a***	***b***	***c***	***d***
a	*c*	*d*	*b*	*a*
b	*d*	*c*	*a*	*b*
c	*b*	*a*	*d*	*c*
d	*a*	*b*	*c*	*d*

I. The identity element of the group is d.
II. The inverse of c is c.
III. The operation # is commutative.

a. I
b. III
c. I, III
d. I, II, III

62. In how many distinguishable ways can a family of five be seated at a circular table with five chairs if Tasha and Mac must be kept separated by at least one chair?

a. 6
b. 12
c. 24
d. 60

63. Which of the following steps were applied to ΔABC?

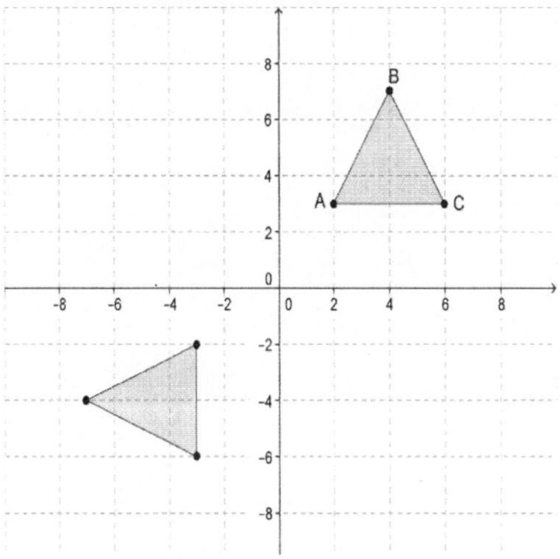

a. Reflection across the x-axis and counterclockwise rotation of 90 degrees about the origin
b. Reflection across the x-axis and counterclockwise rotation of 180 degrees about the origin
c. Reflection across the x-axis and counterclockwise rotation of 270 degrees about the origin
d. Reflection across the y-axis and counterclockwise rotation of 180 degrees about the origin

64. Miss Wise asks her students to work in pairs to construct Venn diagrams which classify rational numbers, irrational numbers, real numbers, and integers. As she walks around the room to observe their progress, which of the following criterion could she use to assess the students' understanding of these sets of numbers?

a. The set of integers should include the other three sets.
b. The set of rational numbers should include the other three sets.
c. The set of irrational numbers should include the other three sets.
d. The set of real numbers should include the other three sets.

65. During a unit on geometry, Ms. Nifong instructs her students to sketch two congruent polygons. Which of the following sketches completes this task correctly?

a. Two rectangles with the same perimeter
b. Two polygons with the same shape
c. Two polygons with the same side lengths
d. Two squares with the same area

66. What is the area of the figure graphed below?

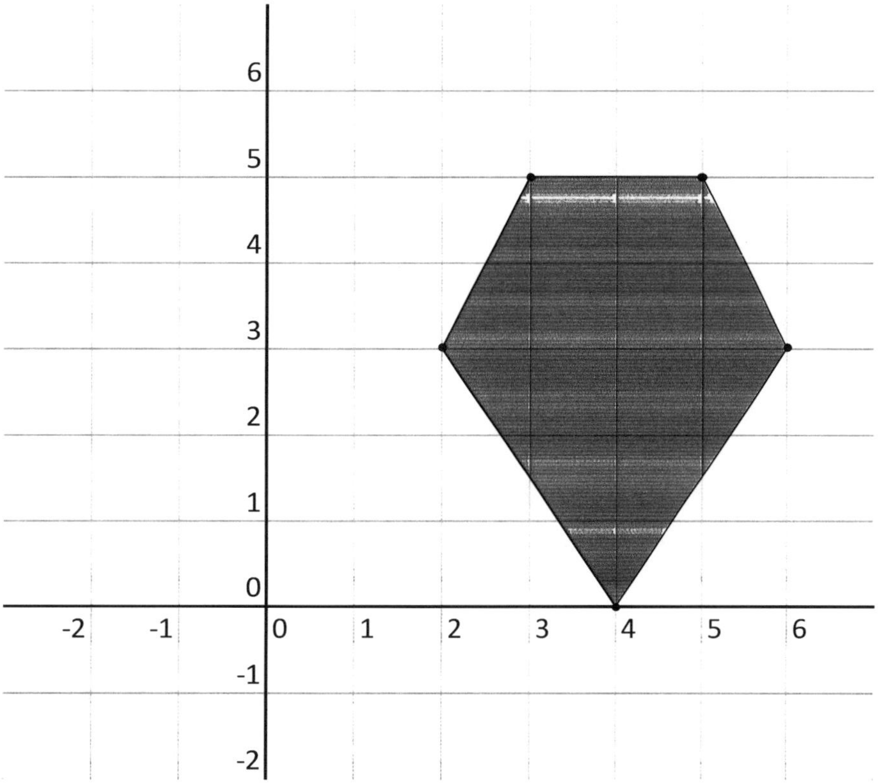

a. 11 units^2
b. 11.5 units^2
c. 12 units^2
d. 12.5 units^2

67. Kayla has a $75 budget to purchase gifts for her colleagues. She wants to buy coffee mugs and note pads. She may purchase a maximum of 30 items. Each coffee mug costs $6 and each note pad costs $3. Which of the following graphs correctly shows the possible combinations of coffee mugs and note pads that she may buy?

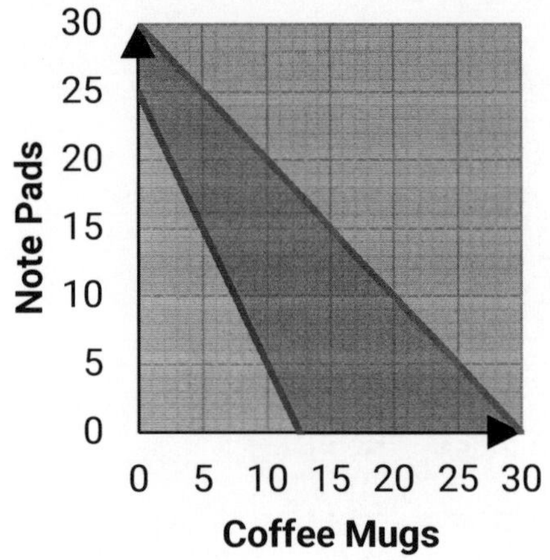

a.

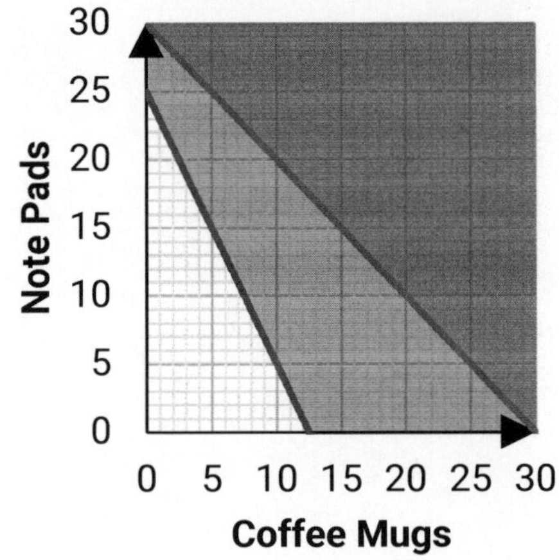

b.

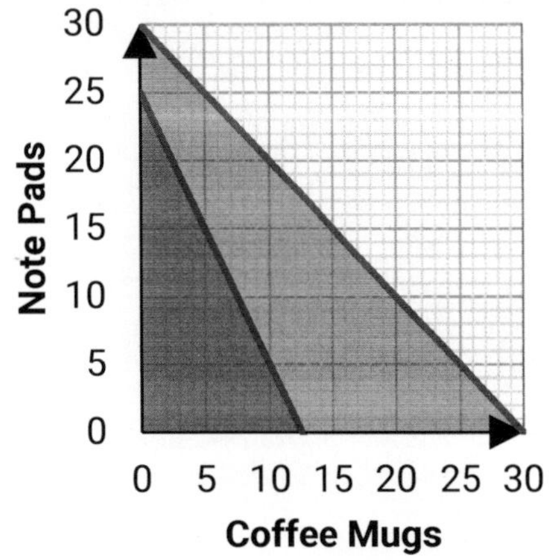

c.

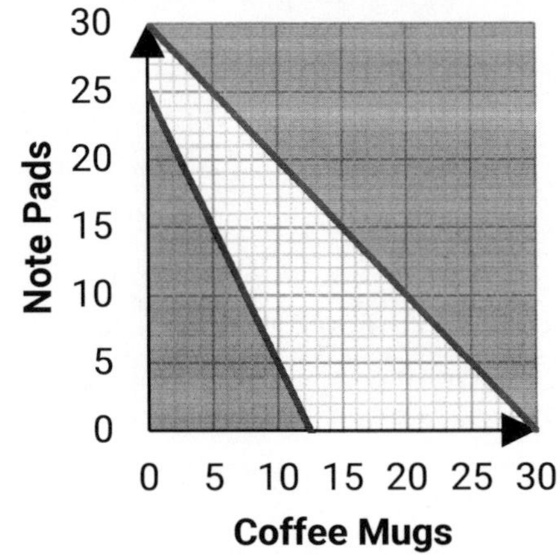

d.

68. What is the constant of proportionality represented by the table below?

x	y
2	−8
5	−20
7	−28
10	−40
11	−44

a. −12
b. −8
c. −6
d. −4

69. Ms. Alejo is teaching a unit on fractions to her third-grade class. Some students are completing an activity in identifying the parts of a fraction. Others are completing an activity on equivalent fractions. Another group of students is completing an activity on adding and subtracting fractions. Which of the following instruction methods describes the various readiness levels Ms. Alejo is incorporating?

a. Collaborative learning
b. Small group instruction
c. Nonlinguistic representations
d. Differentiated instruction

70. During an activity, Mrs. Schwartz instructs her students to place coins into three groups, where each group gets progressively lower in total value. Which of the following students correctly completed this activity?

a. Henry with Group 1: 2 dimes, 2 nickels, and 4 pennies; Group 2: 1 dime, 3 nickels, 2 pennies; Group 3: 2 dimes, 1 nickel, 4 pennies
b. Graham with Group 1: 1 dime, 5 nickels, and 5 pennies; Group 2: 2 dimes, 2 nickels, 8 pennies; Group 3: 1 dime, 2 nickel, 9 pennies
c. Landon with Group 1: 3 dimes, 4 nickels, and 9 pennies; Group 2: 2 dimes, 4 nickels, 3 pennies; Group 3: 1 dime, 9 nickels, 2 pennies
d. Elizabeth with Group 1: 2 dimes, 2 nickels, and 9 pennies; Group 2: 2 dimes, 4 nickels, 1 penny; Group 3: 1 dime, 1 nickel, 7 pennies

71. What is the length of the hypotenuse in the triangle shown below?

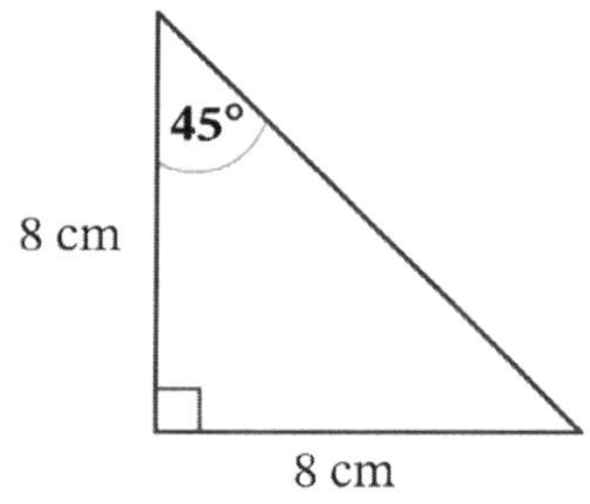

a. 4 cm
b. $8\sqrt{3}$ cm
c. 16 cm
d. $8\sqrt{2}$ cm

72. A cube inscribed in a sphere has a volume of 64 cubic units. What is the volume of the sphere in cubic units?

a. $4\pi\sqrt{3}$
b. $8\pi\sqrt{3}$
c. $32\pi\sqrt{3}$
d. $256\pi\sqrt{3}$

73. Mandy can buy 4 containers of yogurt and 3 boxes of crackers for $9.55. She can buy 2 containers of yogurt and 2 boxes of crackers for $5.90. How much does one box of crackers cost?

a. $1.75
b. $2.00
c. $2.25
d. $2.50

74. Which of the following describes how to find the volume of a regular solid prism?

a. Find the perimeter of the base of the prism and multiply by the height of the prism.
b. Find the area of the base of the prism and multiply by the height of the prism.
c. Find the sum of the areas of the faces and multiply by the length of the prism.
d. Find the sum of the areas of the lateral faces and multiply by the number of faces.

75. $A = \{3, -4, 1\}$ **and** $B = \{0, 5, 9, 2\}$**. What is** $A \cap B$**?**

a. $\{3, -4,1,0,5,9,2\}$
b. $\{-4,2,3\}$
c. $\{0,1,2,3,5,9\}$
d. $\emptyset$

76. Which of these would best illustrate change over time?

a. Pie chart
b. Line graph
c. Box-and-whisker plot
d. Venn diagram

77. Which of the following activities is most appropriate for developing a first-grader's concept of measuring objects?

a. Measuring the height of the pencil sharpener using a meter stick
b. Measuring the length of the chalkboard using a tape measure
c. Measuring the width of their desks using dominoes placed end to end
d. Measuring the circumference of the trash can using a cloth tape

78. The two prisms shown below are similar. What is the measurement of x**?**

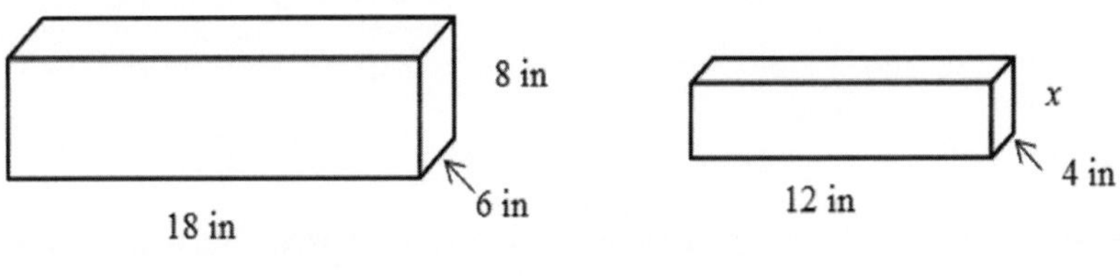

a. $4\frac{3}{4}$ in
b. $5\frac{1}{3}$ in
c. $5\frac{2}{3}$ in
d. $5\frac{3}{4}$ in

79. Kim's current monthly rent is $800. She is moving to another apartment complex, where the monthly rent will be $1,100. What is the percent increase in her monthly rent amount?

a. 25.5%
b. 27%
c. 35%
d. 37.5%

80. A teacher asks her students to find the error in this algebra problem. What is the error?

$$3x + 4x = (2^2 + 1) + 2(2)$$
$$7x = 5 + 2(2)$$
$$7x = 7(2)$$
$$7x = 14$$
$$x = 2$$

a. The student incorrectly added before multiplying.
b. The student incorrectly multiplied before adding.
c. The student incorrectly applied the exponent.
d. The student incorrectly combined like terms.

81. Which of the following is the graph of the equation $y = -4x - 6$?

a.

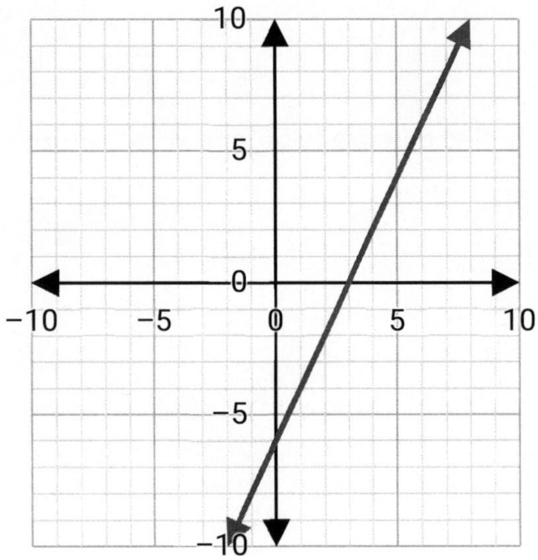

b.

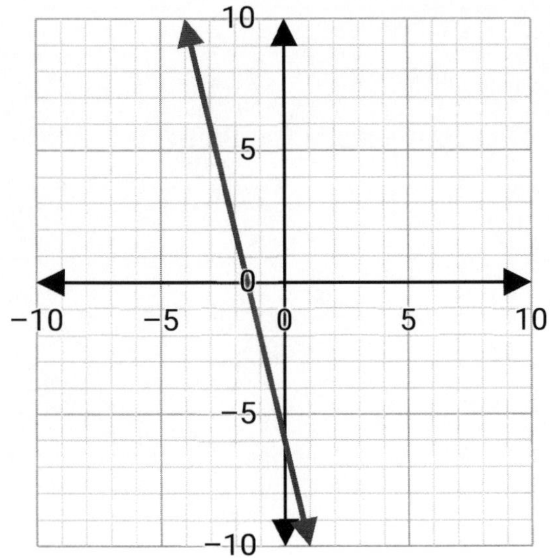

c.

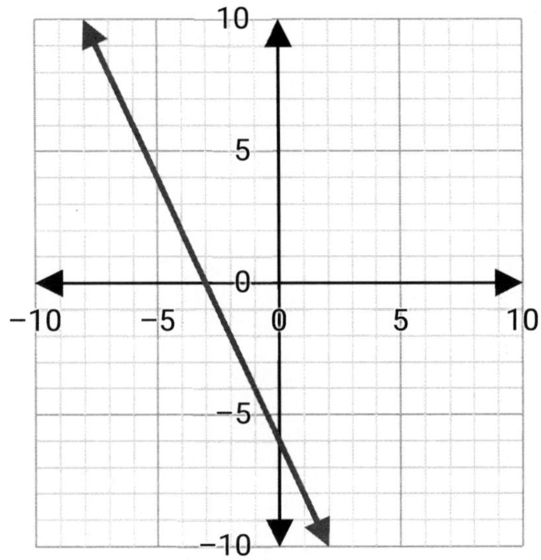

d.

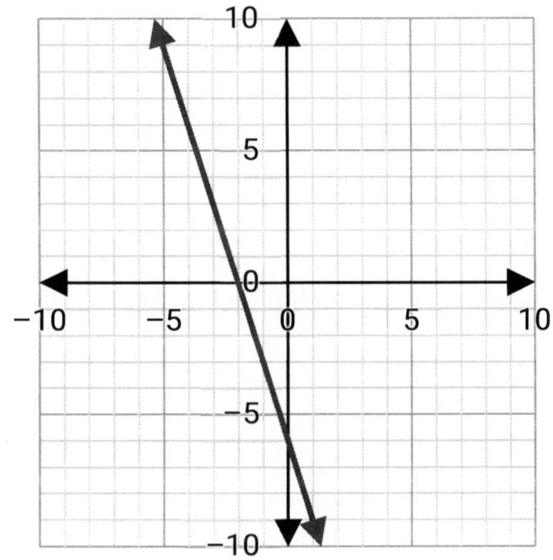

82. Andrea must administer $\frac{1}{12}$ of a medicine bottle to a patient. If the bottle contains $3\frac{4}{10}$ fluid ounces of medicine, how much medicine should be administered?

a. $\frac{17}{60}$ fluid ounces
b. $\frac{15}{62}$ fluid ounces
c. $\frac{3}{19}$ fluid ounces
d. $\frac{17}{67}$ fluid ounces

83. Which of the following options represents equivalency between mathematical expressions?

a. $3 + x + 3x + 3 + x = 5x + 6$
b. $7x - 2x = 9x$
c. $2y + 2y + 2y = 6y^3$
d. $2.5(x + 2) = 2.5x + 2$

84. Kendra uses the pie chart below to represent the allocation of her annual income. Her annual income is $40,000.

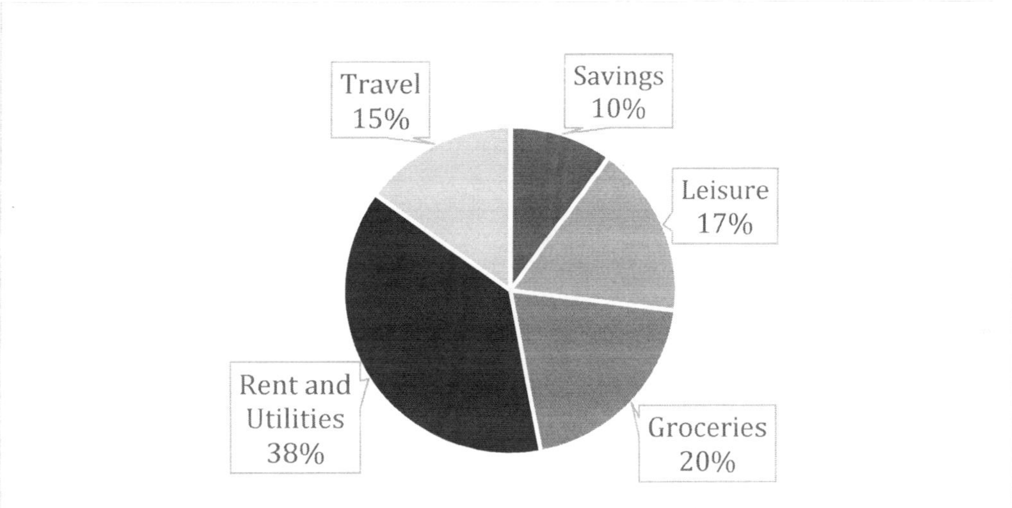

Which of the following statements is true?

a. The amount of money she spends on travel and savings is more than $11,000.
b. The amount of money she spends on rent and utilities is approximately $15,000.
c. The amount of money she spends on groceries and savings is more than $13,000.
d. The amount of money she spends on leisure is less than $5,000.

85. In order to be accepted, amended, or rejected completely, a newly introduced bill is first given to what type of committee?

a. Full committee
b. Conference committee
c. Subcommittee
d. Senate committee

86. Which of the following is NOT true regarding the Virginia Companies?

a. One of these companies, the Virginia Company of Plymouth, made its base in North America.
b. One of these companies, the Virginia Company of London, made its base in Massachusetts.
c. One company had a charter to colonize America between the Hudson and Cape Fear rivers.
d. One company had a charter to colonize America from the Potomac River to north Maine.

87. Why was US industrialization confined to the Northeast until after the Civil War?

a. Because the Civil War delayed the development of water-powered manufacturing
b. Because the Northeast had faster-running rivers than the rivers found in the South
c. Because Slater's first cotton mill with horse-drawn production lost so much money
d. Because the technical innovations for milling textiles had not as yet been invented

88. Unlike slaves, who were considered to be the property of their masters, which of the following was true regarding most indentured servants in colonial times?

a. They received wages for their labor
b. They were generally treated kindly by their employers
c. They were highly educated
d. They voluntarily entered into servitude

89. Which of these was the greatest obstacle to success for the farmers who settled on the Great Plains in the latter part of the nineteenth century?

a. The invention of barbed wire
b. Passage of the Homestead Act
c. Environmental conditions
d. The Grange movement

90. Before the Civil War, to which of the following did Southern states object?

a. An increase in Southern tobacco production
b. An increase in tariffs on Northern manufactured goods
c. An increase in western mining for gold
d. An increase in the voting rights of slaves

91. Which of the following is NOT true about democracy and the formation of the United States?

a. The founding fathers stated in the Constitution that the United States would be a democracy.
b. The Declaration of Independence did not dictate democracy but stated its principles.
c. The United States Constitution stipulated that government be elected by the people.
d. The United States Constitution had terms to protect some, but not all, of the people.

92. According to Karl Marx, which two groups are in continual conflict?

a. Farmers and landowners
b. Workers and owners
c. Kings and nobles
d. Politicians and voters

93. What do the executive, legislative, and judicial branches of government compose?

a. The federal government
b. The democratic process
c. Bicameralism
d. Rule of law

94. Which of the following is NOT correct about the growth of America in the first half of the 19th century?

a. By 1840, two thirds of all Americans resided west of the Allegheny Mountains.
b. The population of America doubled every 25 years during this time period.
c. The trend of westward expansion increased as more people migrated west.
d. Immigration to America from other countries was not substantial prior to 1820.

95. One reason the Articles of Confederation created a weak government was because it limited Congress's ability to do what?

a. Declare war
b. Conduct a census
c. Vote
d. Tax

96. Which of the following ancient civilizations of the Americas lived in Central America?

a. The Incas
b. The Aztecs
c. The Mayans
d. All of these

97. How was the vice president chosen before the 12th Amendment was ratified?

a. The president chose the vice president
b. Congress chose the vice president
c. The vice president came in second in the Electoral College
d. There was no vice president

98. Which list of events is in the correct chronological order?

a. The French and Indian War (Seven Years' War)
The American Revolution
The French Revolution
The War of 1812

b. The American Revolution
The French Revolution
The War of 1812
The French and Indian War (Seven Years' War)

c. The French and Indian War (Seven Years' War)
The French Revolution
The War of 1812
The American Revolution

d. The French and Indian War (Seven Years' War)
The French Revolution
The American Revolution
The War of 1812

99. The Senate and the House of Representatives are an example of:

a. Bicameralism
b. Checks and balances
c. Legislative oversight
d. Federalism

100. If you know the longitude of a city in the United States, what can you determine?

a. The state in which it is located
b. The time zone in which it is located
c. Exactly how far it is from the equator
d. Approximate average winter temperature

101. Which of the following is NOT a direct input in the basic economic concept of a country's gross domestic product (GDP)?

a. The size of its workforce
b. The amount of its capital
c. Technology in place
d. Education of its workforce

102. What was representative democracy likely motivated by?

a. An increase in population
b. Aristocracy
c. The Supreme Court
d. States passing laws that violated federal laws

103. During World War I, which group joined with the Central Powers after it formed?

a. Austria-Hungary
b. Germany
c. Ottoman Empire
d. Italy

104. What is the main purpose of the census?

a. To monitor illegal immigration
b. To apportion seats in the House of Representatives
c. To help determine federal income tax rates
d. To reapportion seats in the United States Senate

105. The impact of a transaction on parties not directly involved in the transaction is known as what?

a. Social cost
b. Social benefit
c. Externality
d. Marginal social cost

106. Which statement is NOT true regarding ancient Greek democracy?

a. Democracy began to develop approximately 500 BC.
b. One of the first, best-known democracies was in Athens.
c. It was a direct democracy, not using any representatives.
d. It was a democracy completely open to all of the public.

Refer to the following for question 107:

During a report on the Industrial Revolution, Mary uses a poster to illustrate cause and effect relationships in the War of 1812.

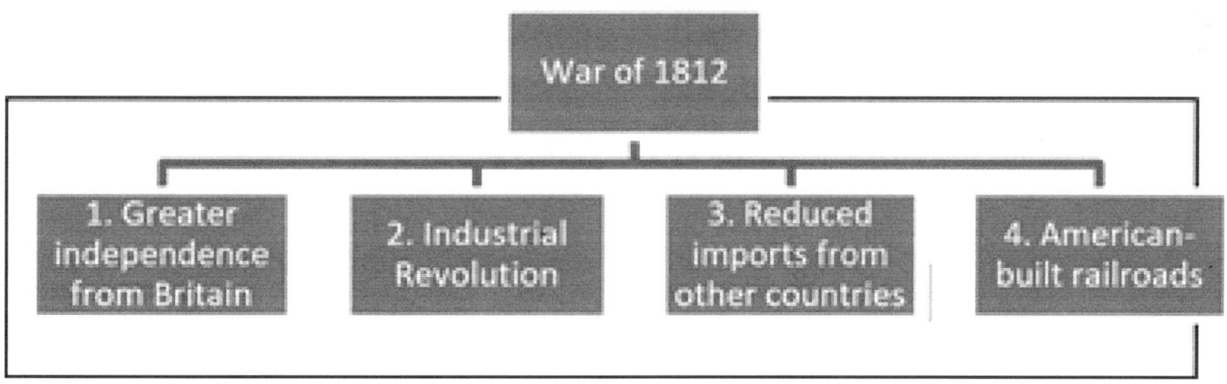

107. Of the following, which should Mary include in her report as more of a cause than an effect of the Industrial Revolution?

a. Emergence of socialism
b. Emergence of capitalism
c. The Romantic movement
d. The Protestant work ethic

108. The Underground Railroad was primarily:

a. A route for abolitionists to smuggle weapons
b. A route for slave owners to traffic slaves
c. A means for slaves to travel to free states
d. A strategy for state control of railway construction

109. What kind of chart would be best for representing the major events of World War I?

a. Timeline
b. Bar graph
c. Pie chart
d. Political map

110. How did World War II influence American society?

a. Consumption decreased in postwar American society.
b. Thousands of people moved to find work in war-related factories.
c. Racially integrated army units helped desegregate American society.
d. Japanese-Americans were banned from serving in the US military.

111. How is a tie broken in the Senate?

a. The president pro tempore casts the deciding vote.
b. The Speaker of the House votes.
c. They vote again.
d. The vice president votes.

112. Which of the following locations would be considered a modern cultural hearth?

a. New York City
b. Baghdad
c. Auckland
d. Edmonton

113. Which of the following is NOT true about Louis Pasteur?

a. He made the first rabies vaccine.
b. He discovered the medical use for penicillin.
c. His experiments advanced the germ theory of disease.
d. He created the first polio vaccine.

114. Which of the following materials has randomly aligned dipoles?

a. A non-magnetic substance
b. An electromagnet
c. A permanent magnet
d. A horseshoe magnet

115. Once a hypothesis has been verified and accepted, it becomes which of the following?

a. A fact
b. A law
c. A conclusion
d. A theory

116. How does the tilt of Earth's axis cause seasons?

a. A hemisphere experiences fall and winter when that half of Earth is tilted away from the sun. It experiences spring and summer when that half of Earth is tilted toward the sun.
b. A hemisphere experiences winter and spring when that half of Earth is tilted away from the sun. It experiences summer and fall when that half of Earth is tilted toward the sun.
c. A hemisphere experiences spring and summer when that half of Earth is tilted away from the sun. It experiences fall and winter when that half of Earth is tilted toward the sun.
d. A hemisphere experiences summer and fall when that half of Earth is tilted away from the sun. It experiences winter and spring when that half of Earth is tilted toward the sun.

117. If a population reaches a maximum size and ceases to grow due to a limited availability of resources, which of the following describes the population?

a. Unstable
b. Shrinking exponentially
c. At carrying capacity
d. Moving towards extinction

118. The center of an atom is called the ____. It is composed of ____.

a. nucleus; protons and neutrons
b. nucleus; protons and electrons
c. electron cloud; electrons and protons
d. electron cloud; electrons and neutrons

119. The volume of water in a bucket is 2.5 liters. When an object with an irregular shape and a mass of 40 grams is fully submerged in the water, the total volume becomes 4.5 liters. What is the density of the object?

a. 0.1 g/L
b. 2 g/L
c. 20 g/L
d. 80 g/L

120. Most organic molecules have all of the following properties EXCEPT:

a. High solubility in water
b. A low melting point
c. Covalent bonds
d. High flammability

121. Which of the following processes is NOT part of the formation of sedimentary rock?

a. Layering
b. Cementation
c. Compaction
d. Heat

122. Which of the following is usually the first form of study in a new area of scientific inquiry?

a. Descriptive studies
b. Controlled experiments
c. Choosing a method and design
d. Identifying dependent and independent variables

123. The specific heat capacity of ice is half as much as that of liquid water. What is the result of this?

a. It takes half the amount of energy to increase the temperature of a 1 kg sample of ice by 1 °C than a 1 kg sample of water.
b. It takes twice the amount of energy to increase the temperature of a 1 kg sample of ice by 1 °C than a 1 kg sample of water.
c. It takes a quarter the amount of energy to increase the temperature of a 1 kg sample of ice by 1 °C than a 1 kg sample of water.
d. It takes the same amount of energy to increase the temperature of a 1 kg sample of ice and a 1 kg sample of water by 1 °C.

124. Which statement best describes the molecular arrangement of a liquid crystal?

a. The molecular arrangement is random in some directions and regular in others.
b. The molecular arrangement is a regular, repeating pattern in all directions.
c. The molecular arrangement is random in all directions.
d. The molecular arrangement is reduced to one layer with a random pattern.

125. Which statement best describes the process of absolute dating?

a. It compares the amount of radioactive material in a rock to the amount that has decayed into another element.
b. It measures the age of a rock by comparing it to fossils found in the same stratigraphic layer as the rock.
c. It measures the amount of daughter elements that have broken down by half.
d. It measures the mass loss of a rock by estimating the amount of material that has eroded due to catastrophic events.

126. The scientific method is a series of steps to accomplish which of the following?

a. Solve a problem
b. Gather information
c. Ask a scientific question
d. Formulate a hypothesis

127. Enzymes play an important role in the processes that help organisms stay healthy and survive. Which of the following best describes enzymes?

a. Enzymes are protein molecules that act as biological catalysts.
b. Enzymes are fat-soluble organic compounds with specific physiological functions.
c. Enzymes are strong acids that break down large biomolecules.
d. Enzymes are lipids that store energy.

128. Which statement accurately describes an electrolysis reaction?

a. A reaction that changes the charge of the atoms
b. A reaction that uses electricity to drive it
c. A reaction that creates electricity as a by-product
d. A reaction that lowers the pH of the substances

129. Which of the following does NOT control the movement of ocean currents?

a. Wind
b. Landmasses
c. Earth's rotation
d. Phase of the Moon

130. The majority of the solar energy that reaches Earth is absorbed by:

a. Glaciers
b. Landmasses
c. Oceans
d. The Earth's atmosphere

131. Electrons with greater amounts of energy are found _______ the nucleus than electrons with less energy.

a. closer to
b. farther from
c. more often inside
d. more randomly around

132. The main function of _______ is to reduce the number of chromosomes to half the number of parent cells.

a. mitosis
b. telophase
c. meiosis I
d. meiosis II

Refer to the following for question 133:

Many fishermen will watch the tide report for the local area and get up very early or stay out late in order to have the best fishing opportunity. One night while out late fishing, a fisherman noticed that the land temperature cooled rapidly, while the ocean water stayed relatively warm.

133. What type of wind was likely created during these conditions?

a. Sea breeze
b. Land breeze
c. Monsoon
d. Trade wind

134. The structure of the Milky Way galaxy is best described as:

a. Spiral
b. Starburst
c. Elliptical
d. Irregular

135. A ball is resting on the front end of a boat. The boat is moving straight forward toward a dock. According to Newton's first law of motion, when the front of the boat hits the dock, how will the ball's motion change with respect to the boat?

a. The ball will remain at rest.
b. The ball will move backward.
c. The ball will move forward.
d. The ball will move upward.

136. In which taxonomic group are organisms MOST alike?

a. Phylum
b. Family
c. Class
d. Order

137. Which statement best explains the importance of recycling and using alternative sources of energy?

a. It will lead to greater production of goods and consumer spending in the future.
b. It will benefit the health and safety of populations and the long-term sustainability of the environment.
c. It will get rid of human disease and end economic warfare in the future.
d. It will allow fossil fuel supplies to be replenished for their continued use in the future.

138. Which of the following planets in our solar system is NOT a gas giant?

a. Saturn
b. Neptune
c. Venus
d. Jupiter

139. A scientist mixes two chemicals together, and they produce a violent reaction, generating considerable heat. Where did the thermal energy come from to heat up the chemicals?

a. The kinetic energy of the molecules in the chemicals
b. Potential energy inherent in the atomic bonds in the molecules of the chemicals
c. It was absorbed from the surrounding air
d. Nowhere; the energy was completely created by the reaction

140. Plants begin to break down the products of photosynthesis through respiration. What is the result of respiration?

a. Water
b. Oxygen and glucose
c. Carbon dioxide and sugar
d. Carbon dioxide and water

141. What property of light explains why a pencil in a glass of water appears to be bent?

a. Reflection
b. Refraction
c. Angle of incidence = angle of reflection
d. Constructive interference

142. Which of the following is an accurate comparison between 3/4 time and 6/8 time, by definition?

a. There is no difference.
b. Both 3/4 time and 6/8 time use three beats per measure.
c. In 3/4 time the quarter note acts as the one-beat unit, while in 6/8 time the eighth note acts as the one-beat unit.
d. 3/4 time uses a quicker tempo.

Refer to the following for question 143:

Ms. Franklin is teaching a second-grade class a lesson on ceramics. While students are engaged in creating their own pieces, Ms. Franklin shows them other students' work.

143. Which of the following would be the most appropriate activity for students at this grade level?

a. Making pinch pots and coil pots
b. Throwing pots using a pottery wheel
c. Making and attaching handles to pots
d. Glazing pots using a kiln

144. What is the fiber-art technique that involves condensing or matting fibers together?

a. Flocking
b. Felting
c. Macramé
d. Plaiting

145. Which of the following activities MOST directly supports a unit on art appreciation and the value and role of art in US society?

a. Having students create a slide show presentation about a famous American artist
b. Asking students to create a timeline showing when famous works of American art were created
c. Taking students on a field trip to an art museum
d. Asking students to write an essay comparing and contrasting the influence that two famous American artists or artworks had on US society

146. What is the relative difference in frequency between these two notes?

a. 1:1
b. 2:1
c. 4:1
d. 8:1

147. A photograph of a small child standing alone in an empty room would have

a. Asymmetrical composition
b. Symmetrical composition
c. Artistic unity
d. Lots of negative space

148. Which of the following factors would plausibly explain two observers' differing evaluations of the same painting?

a. Differing levels of artistic knowledge
b. Different vantage points
c. Different cultural beliefs and values
d. All of the above

149. Which of the following is NOT true of careers in the art industry?

a. The majority of artists are self-employed.
b. Few artists bother earning postsecondary degrees or certificates.
c. Competition is keen for salaried jobs in the art industry.
d. Annual earnings for artists vary widely.

150. Which of the following is MOST appropriate concerning extracurricular activities for student health needs?

a. A student should expect to feel overextended when participating in activities.
b. A student should discontinue an activity if he or she cannot keep up with all things.
c. A student should join only those activities that he or she already knows how to do.
d. A student should consider trying new things but not the time that is available.

Answer Key and Explanations for Test #2

1. C: The question prompt states that Ms. Baird wants to make sure her students understand certain concepts on an individual basis, rather than as a group. This scenario describes a situation in which the students support each other in creating a foundation for the activity. They help each other and are scaffolded by their teacher in determining the main ideas. However, Ms. Baird utilizes the practice of silent reading to ensure that students are practicing the skill of finding supporting evidence on an individual level. She will be able to gauge each student's comprehension levels by checking their notecards after the lesson.

2. C: The goal of a persuasive essay is to convince the reader that the author's position or opinion on a topic is correct. That opinion or position is called the argument. A persuasive essay argues a series of points that are supported by facts and evidence.

3. C: Expository essays are any type of essay in which the writer is providing meaningful information about a topic for the purpose of informing. Most of the topics listed in the example include informational tasks, explaining the process of doing something, such as baking or juggling. Expository essays can use various organizational schemes to help structure the information, such as by comparing and contrasting two things. An expository essay is different from an argumentative essay in that it is not trying to convince the reader of anything, but only trying to inform. Similarly, the purpose of a descriptive essay is to show detail, but not necessarily to inform about how something works.

4. B: Starting in the late 20th century and continuing to today, the current era has been known as the Information Age (as a step forward from the Industrial Age). This is primarily because, with widespread computer and internet use and other innovations in information technology, there are more sources of information and greater output of information than ever before, to such an extent that the amount of information and the power of information technology have caused major shifts in many areas, from how people conduct their lives to how the global economy functions. While some organizations might collect more information that they did before, this is only possible because such information is more readily available now, and it is not necessarily the case that they need the information, so choice A is incorrect. While privacy and the protection of information have come under greater threat recently, they themselves are not more important than they were before, so choice C is incorrect. It is plausible that people are seeking more information about a wider variety of topics than ever before, but this is not the reason that the current era is known as the Information Age, so choice D is incorrect.

5. A: "Conceptual vocabulary" terms are related in meaning and often have complex meanings. For instance, the term *community* may refer simply to a group of people living in close proximity to one another. However, there are many ideas that can be associated with this concept: neighbors, helping, spending time with one another, roles within a community, and so on. Word webs can be used to show a central term and its related concepts, demonstrating the relationship between words based on meaning. Using this type of graphic organizer provides a tangible way to show students that some words have complex meanings and are interconnected with other aspects of language.

6. C: This method is likely to fail, producing students at a Frustration reading level. Those reading below grade level are likely to give up entirely. Those reading at grade level are likely to get frustrated and form habits that will actually slow down their development. Giving students texts that are too far beyond their reach produces frustrated readers. In an effort to succeed, frustrated readers are likely to apply strategies that have worked for them in the past but cannot work in this case because the text is simply beyond them. Looking for contextual clues to understand the meaning of unfamiliar words requires that most of the words in the passage are familiar. Breaking unfamiliar words into individual phonemes or syllables can be effective, but not if the number of such words is excessive. In this case, students below reading level and students at reading level will become frustrated when the skills that have worked for them in the past now fail.

7. D: Asking children to write a list provides them with a visual model that is a side-by-side comparison of the two countries. In creating that visual model, each student first has to organize his or her thoughts mentally, deciding whether each particular item under consideration is shared between both countries or is a difference between them.

8. D: When an online source is in the PDF file format or another file format that has stable pagination, MLA guidelines advise to include applicable page numbers in in-text citations because these numbers are valid and will not change. Therefore, choice D is correct. If an internet source has no pagination, as often happens, the MLA does not advise avoiding the citation, so choice A is incorrect. Rather, it advises simply making the citation without page numbers. Although a printout of an internet source will by necessity have page numbers (for the printed pages), these page numbers will be inconsistent from one printout to another, unlike PDFs. Therefore, the MLA advises not including these page numbers even if you see them, so choice B is incorrect. As already explained, there are cases where an online source will have stable pagination, and the MLA recommends including page numbers in citations of these sources, so choice C is incorrect.

9. A: Basic interpersonal communication skills (BICS) are language skills required in everyday social communication. These are less cognitively demanding, do not involve specialized vocabulary, typically take place in meaningful social contexts, and are necessary for social interaction. Cognitive academic language proficiency (CALP) is formal academic subject content language learning. CALP is more cognitively demanding, involves specialized subject vocabularies, takes place in academic contexts, and is necessary for school success. ELL students typically take 6 months to 2 years to develop adequate BICS, but at least 5-7 years to develop adequate CALP. If they had no formal education in their native languages and/or no second-language acquisition support, development may take 7-10 years.

10. C: These are content-specific words. Because these words are specific to penguins, it's unlikely the students know their meanings. Without understanding what these words mean, the students would not be able to understand the content of the passage they were about to read.

11. B: "Pretty as a picture" is a simile, which is a comparison of two unlike things using the words *like* or *as*. A metaphor is a similar comparison between two unlike things, but metaphors do not use the words *like* or *as*. Synecdoche is a phrase that uses a part to represent the whole of something. For instance, one might refer to "the crown" to refer to a royal family. Finally, a paradox is a statement that appears to contradict itself. All of these are considered figures of speech.

12. A: An introduction should move from broad, general statements about a topic to a focused and specific point regarding the topic. This point is the thesis statement. While the strongest points should come later in the body of an essay, the most attention-grabbing statements should be those in the introduction, as these will serve to engage the reader's interest in the topic and in reading the rest of the essay. Therefore, choice B is incorrect. Starting with focused and specific statements followed by broad and general statements is the opposite of how an introduction should be structured, so choice C is incorrect. Writing experts advise that the technique of beginning an essay with a dictionary definition has become overused and should therefore be avoided, so choice D is incorrect.

13. D: The most practical, thorough, and effective solution is to conduct informal assessments, as well as formal assessments other than the one the school has selected for biannual administration, to obtain continuing data on student phonological development to inform instructional planning, implementation, and adjustments according to student responses. Limiting assessment to the biannual formal test (A) will not provide enough information for individualizing instruction to each student's needs timely enough. Lobbying administrators to change policy (B) could work with some teachers and some administrators, but in many other cases would waste energy and time—and could strain teacher-administrator relations—without succeeding. Using informal assessments continually (C) is a good but not complete solution, whereas using both informal and other formal assessments continually (D) is.

14. A: Phonemic awareness is the ability to recognize sounds within words, so it is a type of phonological awareness. Segmenting words and blending sounds are components of phonemic awareness. Phonological awareness includes an understanding of multiple components of spoken language. The ability to hear individual words within a vocalized stream and the ability to identify spoken syllables are types of phonological awareness.

15. D: Targeted instruction is achieved by assessing areas needing improvement as well as areas of greatest strength for each student, and adjusting instruction to target those areas. This helps to ensure that all members of a class are receiving instruction tailored to their specific needs.

16. B: Tone is the writer's attitude in a given piece of writing, as it is expressed in that writing. Voice can be thought of as the person who the reader "hears"—the particular way an individual writer expresses themselves. Choice B fills in the blanks correctly. Style (C and D) includes both of these and more; it is the effect a writer creates through purposeful use of all the elements of written language, from tone and voice to grammar and structure.

17. A: In both the fictional narrative genre and the nonfictional informational genre, the author will demonstrate some individual writing style; even very factual and objective expositional writing will reveal some personal stylistic characteristics. Labeled diagrams and photos are more likely to be found in informational nonfiction. The majority of books with excitement and drama are fictional narratives (some informational nonfiction books are presented in narrative form and include excitement, especially in children's literature, but these are the minority). Themes and plots are also literary elements associated with fictional narrative.

18. B: Consonant blend refers to a group of consonants in which each letter represents a separate sound.

19. B: A maze test is a specific type of cloze test. In a cloze test, words are deleted, and the reader must supply the missing words using contextual clues and vocabulary that is familiar. A maze test is essentially a multiple-choice application of a cloze test.

20. B: The verbs listed here all refer to taking pieces or parts of information or knowledge and bringing them together to create a whole, and to building relationships among the parts to fit new or different circumstances. Analysis is the opposite of synthesis—breaking information down into its component parts and demonstrating the relationships among those parts. An assignment for analysis would ask the student to compare, distinguish, test, categorize, examine, contrast, or analyze information. Evaluation is making judgments of information based on given criteria, confirming or supporting certain preferences, and persuading the reader. An assignment targeting evaluation would use words like evaluate, predict, appraise, conclude, score, judge, or compare. Application is using knowledge in new contexts. The assignment would ask the student to apply, prepare, practice, use, operate, sketch, calculate, solve, or illustrate.

21. B: According to many academic standards, second graders should be able to determine the meanings of new or unfamiliar words by comparing them to synonyms (words with similar meanings) and antonyms (words with opposite meanings). First graders are expected to use phonics (letter-sound correspondences), word roots, word suffixes, and analogies (A) to decode words for reading. It is expected of third graders to use not only known synonyms and antonyms, but additionally homophones (words sounding the same with different meanings) and homographs (words spelled the same but with different meanings) they know to discern new or unfamiliar word meanings (C). Determining word meanings by referring to word roots, prefixes, suffixes, idiomatic expressions, and familiar diacritical marks used in dictionaries (D) is expected of fourth graders.

22. C: The act of decoding involves first recognizing the sounds individual letters and letter groups make, and then blending the sounds to read the word. A child decoding the word *spin*, for example, would first pronounce *sp/i/n* as individual sound units. She then would repeat the sounds, smoothly blending them. Because decoding involves understanding letters and their sounds, it is sometimes known as the alphabetic principle.

23. D: Based on a Japanese form of poetry, haiku have become popular with students and teachers alike. Reading and writing haiku helps younger students become aware of syllables and helps older students learn about subtleties of vocabulary.

24. B: Assessment is an ongoing process that involves formal testing and a host of other methods. Students are working at any given time in the school year on a multitude of skill sets, and all of these skills are interrelated and developing simultaneously at different rates. It is difficult to provide a complete "snapshot" of a student's abilities, because each student develops in a unique and complex manner. Choice A would only offer insight into a student's reading fluency. Choice C would show how a student could perform on standardized tests; however, many factors such as anxiety and test-taking speed affect those scores. Choice D relies on the teacher to interpret the student's strengths and weaknesses and would require an almost impossible attention to detail. Choice B includes both formal and informal assessments as well as giving insight into writing, vocabulary and other skill sets in a comprehensive portfolio.

25. B: Before beginning fluency instruction, typically not before halfway through the first grade at the earliest, teachers should ensure that students have strong word recognition skills to provide the necessary foundation. Student speed and automaticity in decoding individual words are directly related to developing reading fluency (A): rapid, automatic word decoding is the precursor to fluent reading. Reading fluency not only indicates faster information processing, it also has a direct impact on comprehension (C) because the faster a student can process information, the better the student can comprehend what she reads. When a student must decode words more slowly and less automatically, both reading fluency and comprehension are decreased (D). Slow, conscious decoding does not increase comprehension by being more careful or thoughtful; instead, laborious student efforts to decode separate words for meaning divert the attention they could devote to overall comprehension if they could decode rapidly, effortlessly, and automatically.

26. C: In one minute, a student who misreads one or less than one word per twenty words, or with 95%–100% accuracy, is at an Independent reading level. A student who misreads one or less than one word per ten words, or with 90%–95% accuracy, is at an Instructional level. A student misreading more than one word out of ten, or with less than 90% accuracy, is at a Frustration level.

27. A: The haiku, originating in Japanese poetry and since adopted in English-language poetry, is a short poem of only three lines, often with 17 syllables, with the first and third lines having five syllables and the second line having seven syllables. (In Japanese there are many other rules, which become complicated in comparison to the English version.) Because this syllable pattern is a defining characteristic of English-language haiku, choice A is correct. Haiku are typically unrhymed, so they do not have a rhyme scheme (B). Similarly, they do not employ any regular meter (C). Because haiku are typically 17 syllables or fewer, they do not involve long narratives (D).

28. A: Students are completely capable of understanding and appreciating oral traditions and written texts from other world cultures, as well as those originating from cultures in the students' own community. In fact, introducing a variety of material can increase some students' appreciation of language and literature as it enables them to learn about the world around them. Language skills emerge at a point in most children's development during which students are fascinated with learning new concepts. Introducing a variety of texts also benefits students in a classroom who belong to other cultures; these students are able to learn concepts from texts that represent their family, culture, or country of origin.

29. C: In Choice A, the word prince is capitalized, even though it does not have a suffix. In choice B, the word *multimedia* contains the prefix *multi-*, but no suffix. Choice C contains a word with the root *please*, which also has both a prefix and a suffix. The suffix *-ing* acts as the suffix in *displeasing*, therefore it is correctly capitalized. Choice D correctly has *bookkeeper* capitalized due to the suffix -*er* but neglects to capitalize *examined* even though it also contains a suffix. Choice C is the only correct choice available.

30. A: Most adults can understand the relationship between oral and written language: components of oral language have representational symbols that can be written and decoded. However, most normally-developing children acquire spoken language first and begin to develop reading and writing skills as they approach school-age. Many children are first exposed to the concept of written language when an adult introduces books or other written texts. However, a child's ability to read and write develops over time and is dependent on the development of physiological processes such as hearing, sight, and fine motor skills for writing. Written language development also typically requires direct instruction. Most children must be taught to read and write and rarely learn these skills simply by observing others.

31. D: Phonemes are the smallest units of sound in words. In this activity, students are replacing one phoneme with another, which is known as phoneme substitution. Alliteration refers to a series of words in which most words begin with the same sound. Segmenting refers to breaking a word down into its individual sounds, or phonemes. Onset and rime blending involve blending the beginning sound of a word with the rest of the word.

32. D: Classrooms will most always consist of students at different levels of ability. The physical and psychological processes needed for reading evolve simultaneously over time and do so at different rates for each individual. No two students will match up perfectly with respect to language skills. Language skills also incorporate a variety of other processes, including speaking, listening, thinking, viewing, writing, and reading. By pairing direct instruction with various types of cognitive processes, all students receive varied instruction and will make progress. By being introduced to different types of text, students will develop skills according to their own strengths at that particular time.

33. B: Manipulatives are three-dimensional concrete objects that students can not only look at but also manipulate, as the name indicates (e.g., touch, move, rearrange, dismantle, reassemble).

Examples may be three-dimensional objects, demonstrations, or (more often) verbal descriptions given orally, printed, or written. Graphic organizers are diagrams (e.g., Venn diagrams), charts, timelines, concept maps, word webs, etc., which are two-dimensional, visual, graphic materials. Charts, tables, and graphs, though less pictorial and conceptual and more linear and numerical than graphic organizers, are also two-dimensional in print, online, or on screen.

34. D: CVC words, like dog, sit, and leg, are composed of a consonant, a vowel, and a consonant. To learn to read them, students must be familiar with the letters used and their sounds. A teacher can present a word like *sit* to students who also know the consonants *b/f/h/p* and ask them to create a word family of other CVC words. The students will be able to read *bit, fit, hit,* and *pit* because they are similar to the word *sit* that they have just learned.

35. B: Researchers find that both learners a native language (L1 learners) and a learners of a second-language (L2 learners) go through all stages of language acquisition. However, L2 learners are often urged by teachers and others to skip the so-called "silent period" more than their L1 learner counterparts, who are acquiring their native language. Therefore, choice B is correct. Because both L1 learners and L2 learners have been found to go through all the stages, choices A and C are incorrect. L2 learners are not likely to undergo the third stage later, but sooner than or at a similar time as L1 learners, so choice D is incorrect.

36. C: There is currently a wide variety of technology resources available that can support class instruction. However, teachers must choose carefully in order to ensure that the technology is useful and relevant to the intended learning outcomes for the class. The language lab described allows students to experience text through both listening and reading, thereby utilizing different processes in the brain. The interactive modules also support decoding and comprehension skills that go along with the texts. This use of technology reinforces important skills in a way that will be unique and interesting for the students.

37. B: Based on Charles Read's (1975) research into invented and phonetic spelling, Richard Gentry (1982, 2006, 2010) identified five phases of spelling. *Precommunicative*: Alphabetic symbols without letter-sound correspondences, complete alphabet knowledge, spelling directionality, or uppercase and lowercase letter distinctions. *Semiphonetic*: Letter-sound correspondence understanding emerges; students frequently spell words with single letters or abbreviated syllables. *Phonetic*: Not all spellings follow standard conventions, but students systematically represent all phonemes with letters. Misspellings are typically accurate in terms of articulatory placement (*e* for short *i*, *a* for short *e*, *i* for short *o*, etc.) *Transitional*: Students move from phonetic to conventional, visual spellings, informed by their growing understanding of word structure. "Higheked" for "hiked" and "egul" for "eagle" are examples of their more approximate spellings. *Correct*: Students have learned the fundamental rules of English orthography, including irregular and alternative spellings, silent consonants, prefixes and suffixes, etc., and can identify misspellings.

38. B: Context clues offer insight into the probable meaning of unfamiliar words.

39. B: The term standard English refers to a form of English used in an English-speaking country that is reflected in dictionaries and grammar books, taught to English language learners, used in published writing, and so on. Because the rules of standard English are adhered to mainly in edited writing, choice B is correct. Standard English actually includes and allows for a range of dialects, which is exemplified by the fact that what is considered a standard English varies between English-speaking countries, so choice A is incorrect. Standard English is not universal; different English-speaking countries have different standard Englishes, so choice C is incorrect. Choice D is incorrect because edited and published writing generally adheres to some form of standard English.

40. C: All private and public schools will provide some sort of curriculum guidance, which usually takes the form of a list of concepts that must be covered within a certain time frame. Teachers must use this provision as a guideline for planning instruction. However, with time and creativity, teachers can bring these concepts to life using various types of material (e.g., oral, written, media, and performance) and engaging instructional methods. Teachers can also find ways to integrate instruction and concepts with teachers of other subjects to ensure that students understand that language skills are not only interrelated, but also applicable to all areas of learning.

41. D: Expectations include interpreting and understanding visual imagery, meanings, and messages; analyzing and critiquing the importance of visual media; and evaluating the ways that various media inform and influence people. Developing and organizing ideas from the environment is an expectation, but not from the English Language Arts subject area; it is an expectation for middle school students in the Fine Arts subject area.

42. A: Syllable types include closed, open, silent *e*, vowel team, vowel-*r*, and consonant-*le*. A closed syllable ends with a consonant, such as *cat*. Open syllables end with a vowel, such as *he*. Vowel team syllables contain two vowels working together, such as *main.* Vowel-*r* syllables such as *er* and *or* frequently occur as suffixes. Consonant-*le* syllables also typically occur as suffixes, such as *battle* or *terrible.*

43. C: Neologisms (from *neo-* meaning "new"), also known as "creative coinages," are new words sometimes invented by people which then become parts of our vocabulary. The word *noob* refers to a person new to a context. It was first largely used in the 1960s and 1970s to describe the new man in a military unit during the Vietnam War. Blending is another way new words come into our language; for example, *moped* is a blend of the respective first syllables of *motor* and *pedal*. Conversion, also called functional shift, changes a word's part of speech. For example, the common nouns *network*, *microwave*, and *fax*, along with the proper noun *Google* have all been converted to verbs in modern usage. Onomatopoeia means words that imitate associated sounds, such as *meow* and *click*.

44. B: The teacher used an informal reading inventory to gain insight into the students' abilities in a larger group setting. While some informal reading inventories, or IRIs, are administered between one teacher and one student, these inventories usually work best in a group setting. The benefit of this type of assessment is that it provides insight within the context of an entire class or large group in a short period of time. This assessment does not provide specific or generalized information about the students' progress, but rather allows the teacher to gauge her students' needs at any given point during instruction.

45. A: Norm-referenced tests compare student scores to the average scores of a normative sample of similar students that represents the target population. Informal reading inventories (B) use graded word lists, reading passages from authentic texts, and comprehension questions to identify student reading levels, strengths, and instructional needs rather than comparing student scores to normative group scores. Curriculum-based assessments (C) test student knowledge of the specific material included in the school's curriculum rather than comparing scores. Criterion-referenced tests (D) compare student performance against pre-established criteria for mastery of specific skills, not other students' performance.

46. D: Word recognition is required for reading fluency and is important to all readers, but it is especially so to English Language Learners and students with reading disabilities. It can be effectively taught through precisely calibrated word study instruction designed to provide readers with reading and writing strategies for successful word analysis.

47. B: When adults or other skilled readers take time to read aloud to students, they can model (or demonstrate) what it means to read fluently. Students are still learning about grammar, spelling, decoding, comprehending, speaking, and listening. Therefore, it can be difficult for them to read aloud consistently with appropriate speed, accuracy, and inflection since there are multiple cognitive processes taking place in the student's brain. By listening to an experienced reader, students will better understand how fluent reading is intended to sound and how fluency can affect comprehension in reading or listening.

48. A: The probability that the dart will land in the inner circle is equal to the ratio of the area of inner circle to the area of the outer circle, or $\frac{\pi(3)^2}{\pi(6)^2}$. This reduces to $\frac{1}{4}$.

49. B: The volume of a sphere may be calculated using the formula $V = \frac{4}{3}\pi r^3$, where r represents the radius. Substituting 3.5 for r gives $V = \frac{4}{3}\pi(3.5)^3$, which simplifies to $V \approx 179.6 \text{ in}^3$.

50. A: The vertical line of symmetry is represented by an equation of the form $x = a$. The horizontal line of symmetry is represented by an equation of the form $y = b$. One line of symmetry occurs at $x = -4$. The other line of symmetry occurs at $y = 6$.

51. D: To draw a box-and-whisker plot from the data, find the median, quartiles, and upper and lower limits.

3|6 799
4|2|3889
5|0|11158|
6|0 0123

Key
2|123 = 21, 22, 23

The median is $\frac{50+51}{2} = 50.5$, the lower quartile is $\frac{42+43}{2} = 42.5$, and the upper quartile is $\frac{58+60}{2} = 59$. The box of the box-and-whisker plot goes through the quartiles, and a line through the box represents the median of the data. The whiskers extend from the box to the lower and upper limits, unless there are any outliers in the set. In this case, there are no outliers, so the box-and-whisker plot in choice A correctly represents the data set.

To draw a pie chart, find the percentage of data contained in each of the ranges shown. There are four out of twenty numbers between 30 and 39, inclusive, so the percentage shown in the pie chart for that range of data is $\frac{4}{20} \times 100\% = 20\%$; there are five values between 40 to 49, inclusive, so the percentage of data for that sector is $\frac{5}{20} \times 100\% = 25\%$; $\frac{6}{20} \times 100\% = 30\%$ of the data is within the range of 50–59, and $\frac{5}{20} \times 100\% = 25\%$ is within the range of 60–69. The pie chart shows the correct percentage of data in each category.

To draw a cumulative frequency histogram, find the cumulative frequency of the data.

Range	Frequency	Cumulative frequency
30–39	4	4
40–49	5	9
50–59	6	15
60–69	5	20

The histogram shows the correct cumulative frequencies. Therefore, all of the graphs represent the data set.

52. B: Rate in miles per hour can be expressed as, mph $= \frac{\text{distance in miles}}{\text{time in hours}}$. So, Zeke's driving speed on the way to Atlanta and home from Atlanta in mph can be expressed as $\frac{d}{3}$ and $\frac{d}{2}$, respectively, where d is the distance between Zeke's house and his destination. Since Zeke drove 20 mph faster on his way home, (speed home) − (speed to store) = 20. Substitute Zeke's speeds and solve for d.

$$\frac{d}{2} - \frac{d}{3} = 20$$

$$6\left(\frac{d}{2} - \frac{d}{3} = 20\right)$$
$$3d - 2d = 120$$
$$d = 120$$

Since the distance between Zeke's house and the store in Atlanta is 120 miles, Zeke drove a total distance of 240 miles in five hours. Therefore, his average speed was $\frac{240\text{ miles}}{5\text{ hours}} = 48$ mph.

53. B: All regular polygons have rotational symmetry. The angle of rotation is the smallest angle by which the polygon can be rotated such that it maps onto itself; any multiple of this angle will also map the polygon onto itself. The angle of rotation for a regular polygon is the angle formed between two lines drawn from consecutive vertices to the center of the polygon. Since the vertices of a regular polygon lie on a circle, for a regular polygon with n sides, the angle of rotation measures $\frac{360°}{n}$. Therefore, a square has rotational symmetry about the angle 90° and its multiples. A regular hexagon has rotational symmetry about the angle 60° and its multiples. A regular octagon has rotational symmetry about 45° and its multiples. And a regular decagon has rotational symmetry about 36° and its multiples. Since 120° is a multiple of 60°, the correct answer is a regular hexagon.

54. D: The original cost may be represented by the equation $45 = x - 0.25x$ or $45 = 0.75x$. Dividing both sides of the equation by 0.75 gives $x = 60$.

55. C: The volume of a pyramid may be calculated using the formula $V = \frac{1}{3}Bh$, where B represents the area of the base and h represents the height. Since the base is a square, the area of the base is equal to 6^2, or 36 square inches. Substituting 36 for B and 9 for h gives $V = \frac{1}{3}(36)(9)$, which simplifies to $V = 108$ cubic inches.

56. D: Students using cardboard manipulatives is the most learner-centered activity since it includes hands-on activities with the use of manipulatives. Watching a video and completing a worksheet are learner-centered but do not include hands-on activities. The teacher working subtraction problems on the whiteboard is teacher-centered.

57. D: This problem can be represented using the proportion $\frac{\textit{number of wins}}{\textit{total games}} = \frac{\textit{number of wins}}{\textit{total games}}$. If the ratio of wins to losses is 2 : 1, then the ratio of wins to total games is 2 : 3. The proportion to determine the number of wins is $\frac{x}{36} = \frac{2}{3}$.

58. D: This sequence lists the sum of the squares of natural numbers and 1. For example, $1^2 + 1$ is 2, and $2^2 + 1$ is 5. The next number in the sequence can be determined squaring 5 and adding 1, $5^2 + 1$, which is 26. Note also that the differences between consecutive numbers in the sequence are consecutive odd integers starting at 3. For example, $2 + 3$ is $5, 5 + 5$ is 10, and $10 + 7$ is 17, so the next number in the sequence is $17 + 9$, or 26.

59. C: As they are a pair of alternate exterior angles, ∠g and ∠c are congruent.

60. D: The numbers in this sequence progress according to a pattern. Each progressing number can be expressed by the equation $x + 2 = n$, where x is the difference between the previous two numbers and n is the number added to the previous number, to yield the progressing number. For instance, the difference in 24 and 16 is 8. By adding 2 to 8, you know that you must add 10 to 24 in order to yield 34. In the next part of the sequence, $x = 10$ and $n = 12$. $34 + 12 = 46$, the next number in the sequence. Therefore, by following this pattern, you would add 16 to 60, which results in 76.

61. D: The identity element is d since $d\#a = a\#d = a, d\#b = b\#d = b, d\#c = c\#d = c$, and $d\#d = d$. The inverse of element c is c since $c\#c = d$, the identity element. The operation # is commutative because $a\#b = b\#a$, $a\#c = c\#a$, etc. Rather than check that the operation is commutative for each pair of elements, note that elements in the table display symmetry about the diagonal elements; this indicates that the operation is indeed commutative.

#	*a*	*b*	*c*	*d*
a	*c*	*d*	*b*	*a*
b	*d*	*c*	*a*	*b*
c	*b*	*a*	*d*	*c*
d	*a*	*b*	*c*	*d*

62. B: One way to approach this problem is to first consider the number of arrangements of the five members of the family if Tasha (T) and Mac (M) must sit together. Treat them as a unit seated in a fixed location at the table; then arrange the other three family members (A, B, and C):

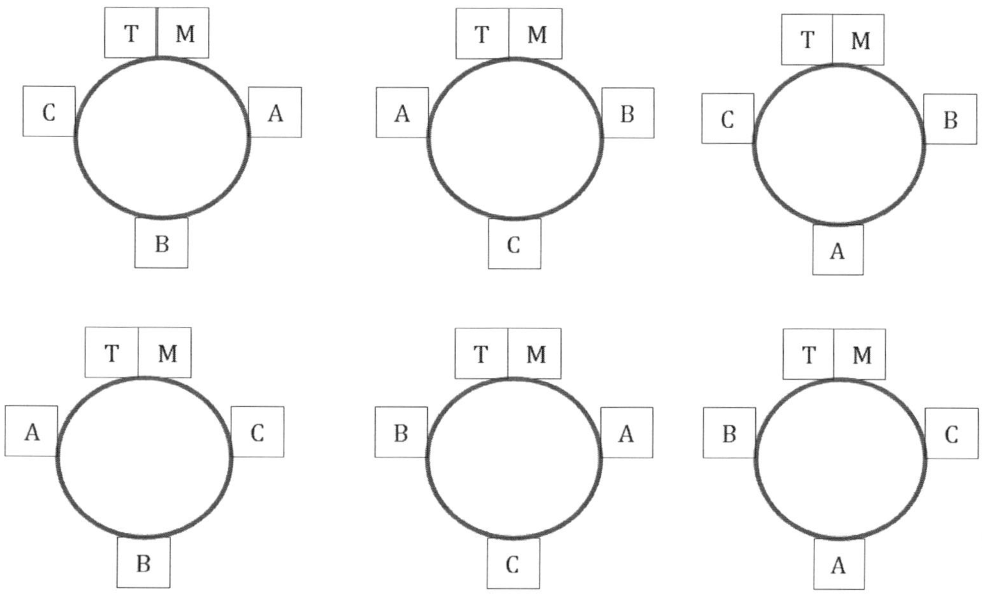

There are six ways to arrange four units around a circle as shown. Any other arrangement would be a rotation in which the elements are in the same order and would therefore not be a unique arrangement. Of course, Mac and Tasha are not actually a single unit. They would still be sitting beside each other if they were to trade seats, so there are 12 arrangements in which the two are seated next to one another. In all other arrangements of the five family members, they are separated. Therefore, to find the number of arrangements in which Tasha and Mac are *not* sitting together, subtract 12 from the possible arrangement of five units around a circle. There are $(n-1)!$ ways to arrange n units around a circle for $n > 1$. So, $(5-1)! - 12 = 24 - 12 = 12$.

63. C: A reflection across the x-axis will result in a triangle with vertices at $(2,-3)$, $(4,-7)$, and $(6,-3)$. A rotation of 270 degrees counterclockwise is denoted by the following: $(x,y) \rightarrow (y,-x)$. Thus, a rotation of the reflected triangle by 270 degrees will result in a figure with vertices at $(-3,-2)$, $(-7,-4)$, and $(-3,-6)$. The transformed triangle indeed has these coordinates as its vertices.

64. D: Real numbers include all rational and irrational numbers. Rational numbers include all integers. The set of real numbers include the other three sets.

65. D: Congruent figures have the same shape and the same size. Two squares have the same shape. If the areas are the same, they also have the same size and are congruent. Choice A is incorrect because two rectangles can have the same perimeter but not the same shape. Choice B is the incorrect because two polygons of the same shape are not necessarily the same size. Choice C is incorrect because two polygons can have the same side lengths but different shapes. Therefore, the correct answer is choice D.

66. C: The area of a trapezoid may be calculated using the formula, $A = \frac{1}{2}(b_1 + b_2)h$. Thus, the area of the trapezoid is represented as $A = \frac{1}{2}(4+2)(2)$, which simplifies to $A = 6$. The area of the triangle is represented as $A = \frac{1}{2}(4)(3)$, which also simplifies to $A = 6$. Thus, the total area is 12 square units.

67. C: The situation may be modeled by the system of inequalities $\begin{cases} 6x + 3y \leq 75 \\ x + y \leq 30 \end{cases}$ where x is the number of coffee mugs and y is the number of note pads. Some algebraic manipulation gives us the inequalities in slope-intercept form: $\begin{cases} y \leq -2x + 25 \\ y \leq -x + 30 \end{cases}$. All four choices graph these lines correctly, but only choice C correctly shades just the region that is below both lines, indicating that both conditions are met.

68. D: The constant of proportionality is equal to the slope. Using the points, $(2, -8)$ and $(5, -20)$, the slope may be written as $\frac{-20-(-8)}{5-2}$, which equals -4.

69. D: Ms. Alejo is using different activities to meet the various readiness levels of her students. This aspect is described as differentiated instruction. Collaborative learning and small group instruction describe the aspect that the students are in groups. The question does not address nonlinguistic representations, such as charts and visual aids. Therefore, the correct answer is choice D.

70. B: Graham has placed Group 1 with 40¢, Group 2 with 38¢, and Group 3 with 29¢. Henry has placed Group 1 with 34¢, Group 2 with 27¢, and Group 3 with 29¢. Landon has placed Group 1 with 59¢, Group 2 with 43¢, and Group 3 with 57¢. Elizabeth has placed Group 1 with 39¢, Group 2 with 41¢, and Group 3 with 22¢.

71. D: The triangle is a 45-45-90 right triangle. Thus, if each leg is represented by x, the hypotenuse is represented by $x\sqrt{2}$. Thus, the hypotenuse is equal to $8\sqrt{2}$ cm.

72. C: The center of the sphere is shared by the center of the cube, and each of the corners of the cube touches the surface of the sphere. Therefore, the diameter of the sphere is the line that passes through the center of the cube and connects one corner of the cube to the opposite corner. In the illustration below, notice that the diameter d of the sphere can be represented as the hypotenuse of a right triangle with a short leg measuring 4 units. (Since the volume of the cube is 64 cubic units, each of its sides measures $\sqrt[3]{64} = 4$ units.) The long leg of the triangle is the diagonal of the base of the cube.

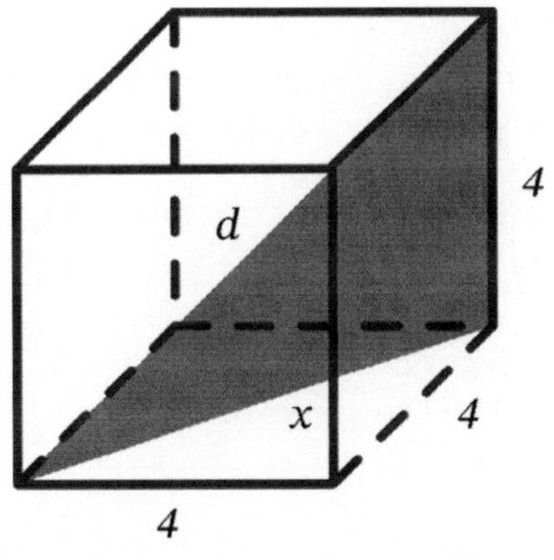

The length of the long leg can be found using the Pythagorean theorem:

$$x^2 = 4^2 + 4^2 = 32$$
$$x = \sqrt{32} = 4\sqrt{2}$$

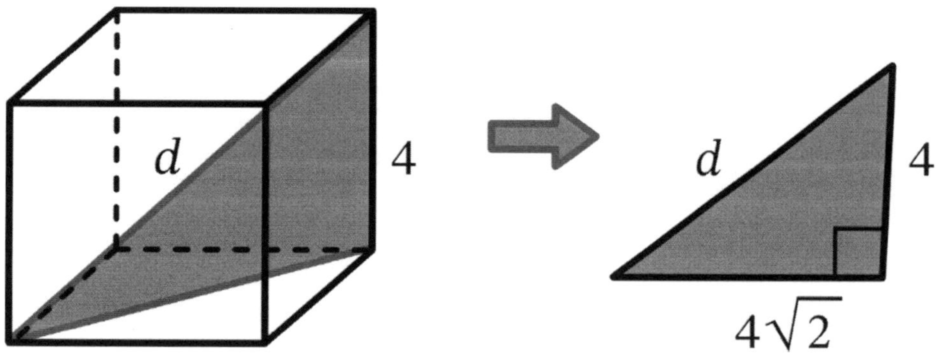

Use the Pythagorean theorem again to find d, the diameter of the sphere:

$$d^2 = \left(4\sqrt{2}\right)^2 + 4^2 = 32 + 16 = 48$$
$$d = \sqrt{48} = 4\sqrt{3}$$

To find the volume of the sphere, use the formula $V = \frac{4}{3}\pi r^3$. Since the radius r of the sphere is half the diameter, $r = 2\sqrt{3}$, and $V = \frac{4}{3}\pi(2\sqrt{3})^3 = \frac{4}{3}\pi\left(24\sqrt{3}\right) = 32\pi\sqrt{3}$ cubic units.

73. C: The situation may be modeled by this system of equations:

$$\begin{cases} 4y + 3c = 9.55 \\ 2y + 2c = 5.90 \end{cases}$$

Multiplying the bottom equation by −2 gives:

$$\begin{cases} 4y + 3c = 9.55 \\ -4y - 4c = -11.80 \end{cases}$$

Adding the two equations gives $-c = -2.25$, or $c = 2.25$. Thus, one box of crackers costs $2.25.

74. B: A regular solid prism is a solid, three-dimensional shape which has length, width, and height. The bases are of the same shape, and the shape of the other faces depend on the shape of the bases. The volume of a regular solid prism can be determined by multiplying the area of the base by the height of the prism.

75. D: The intersection of the two sets is empty, denoted by the symbol, ∅. There are not any elements common to both sets.

76. B: A line graph is often used to show change over time. A Venn diagram shows the relationships among sets. A box-and-whisker plot displays how numeric data are distributed throughout the range. A pie chart shows the relationship of parts to a whole.

77. C: Students in first grade are generally in Piaget's preoperational stage but are making the transition to the concrete operational stage. In the preoperational stage, children are beginning to think symbolically about concrete objects, but are unlikely to think abstractly. In an activity to develop understanding of measurement, it is best to use concrete, manipulative objects and to avoid measurement tasks involving conservation, as this concept is developed in later stages. Measuring the height of a pencil sharpener with a meter stick and measuring the length of a chalkboard with a tape measure are likely achievable for first graders, but are unlikely to give students the stimulation of individual manipulation with concrete objects. A tape measure would only allow one or two students to participate at a time. Furthermore, it may be beneficial for young children to develop an understanding of units by using various non-standard units. Measuring the circumference of a trash can is also probably developmentally inappropriate as it involves some understanding of later geometry concepts such as circumference and may be confusing to first-graders as they should not understand conservation at this point. Having students measure their desks with units such as dominos is an excellent activity for first graders, as it allows students to work individually with manipulatives and allows them to interact with non-standard units.

78. B: Since the figures are similar, the following proportion may be written and solved for x.

$$\frac{6}{4} = \frac{8}{x}$$
$$6x = 4 \times 8$$
$$6x = 32$$
$$x = \frac{32}{6} = 5\frac{2}{6} = 5\frac{1}{3}$$

Therefore, the measure of x is $5\frac{1}{3}$ in.

79. D: This problem can be solved using the percent change formula: $\%\ change = \frac{new - old}{old} \times 100\%$. Thus, the percentage increase is represented as $\%\ change = \frac{1{,}100 - 800}{800} \times 100\% = 37.5\%$.

80. A: In the third line of the problem, the student incorrectly added the 5 and 2 rather than multiplying 2(2). According to the order of operations, the student should multiply before adding.

81. B: The equation $y = -4x - 6$ is in slope-intercept form, $y = mx + b$, where m is the slope and b is the y-intercept. All four graphs show the correct y-intercept, −6, but only one shows the correct slope, −4. The slope of a line can be found by picking any two points (x_1, y_1) and (x_2, y_2) on the line and calculating $m = \frac{y_2 - y_1}{x_2 - x_1}$. For choice B, we can choose points $(0, -6)$ and $(-2, 2)$, which gives us $m = \frac{2-(-6)}{-2-0} = -4$. None of the other graphs have a slope of −4.

82. A: The amount to be administered may be written as $\frac{1}{12} \times \frac{34}{10}$, which equals $\frac{17}{60}$. Thus, she should administer $\frac{17}{60}$ fluid ounces of medicine.

83. A: $3 + x + 3x + 3 + x = 5x + 6$ correctly shows how the combination of like terms on the left side of the equation results in the expression on the right side of the equation. $7x - 2x = 9x$ incorrectly combines like terms by adding the coefficients rather than subtracting them. $2y + 2y + 2y = 6y^3$ incorrectly adds the exponents of like terms instead of just adding the coefficients of like terms. $2.5(x + 2) = 2.5x + 2$ incorrectly distributes the 2.5 across the parentheses by neglecting to multiply the 2.5 with the last term in the expression.

84. B: The amount she spends on rent and utilities is equal to 0.38($40,000), or $15,200, which is approximately $15,000.

85. C: A bill is usually first reviewed by the appropriate subcommittee. The subcommittee can accept the bill, amend the bill, or reject the bill. If the subcommittee accepts or amends the bill, they send it to the full committee for review. Expert witnesses and testimony are all part of committee review.

86. B: The Virginia Company of London was based in London, not Massachusetts. It had a charter to colonize American land between the Hudson and Cape Fear rivers. The other Virginia Company was the Virginia Company of Plymouth, which was based in the American colony of Plymouth, Massachusetts. It had a charter to colonize North America between the Potomac River and the northern boundary of Maine. Both Virginia Companies were joint-stock companies, which had often been used by England for trading with other countries.

87. B: US industrialization was confined to the Northeast until after the Civil War because the Northeast had faster-running rivers than the South. The earliest American factories used horse-drawn machines. When waterpower was developed and proved superior, the Northeast's faster rivers were more suited to water-powered mills than the South's slower rivers. The war did not delay the development of waterpower. Waterpower was developed before the Civil War in the late 1790s. Steam power, a more efficient alternative to waterpower, was developed after the Civil War and eventually replaced waterpower. With steam-powered engines, industry could spread to the South, since steam engines did not depend on rapidly running water like water-powered engines. While British emigré Samuel Slater's first cotton mill using horse-drawn production did lose a lot of money, this was not a reason for industrial delay. In fact, Slater's Beverly Cotton Manufactory in Massachusetts, the first American cotton mill, in spite of its financial problems, was successful in both its volume of cotton production and in developing the water-powered technology that ultimately would succeed the horse-drawn method. Slater's second cotton mill in Pawtucket, Rhode Island, was water-powered. Industrial delay was not because milling technology had not yet been invented. Slater learned of new textile manufacturing techniques as a youth in England, and he brought this knowledge to America in 1789.

88. D: Indentured servants agreed to work for a set period of time in exchange for transportation to the New World and such basic necessities as food and shelter. They did not receive wages and were generally not highly-educated people. Employers often viewed indentured servants with scorn and treated them as harshly as they treated slaves.

89. C: Nature imposed great hardships on farmers. Drought, wind, fires, blizzards, and subzero temperatures made life on the plains very difficult and dangerous. The invention of barbed wire in 1874 allowed farmers to keep livestock from damaging their crops. The Homestead Act of 1862 encouraged settlement of the west and made land available to some 600,000 homesteaders. Founded in 1867, the Grange united farmers in their effort to regulate storage and shipping costs and generally protect their own interests.

90. B: Southern states provided raw materials that were manufactured into commodities in Northern states. Southerners resented paying taxes to Northern states for these products (textiles, furniture, etc.).

91. A: It is not true that the founding fathers specifically stated in the Constitution that the United States would be a democracy. The founding fathers wanted the new United States to be founded on principles of liberty and equality, but they did not specifically describe these principles with the term *democracy*. Thus, the Declaration of Independence, like the Constitution after it, did not stipulate a democracy, although both did state the principles of equality and freedom. The Constitution also provided for the election of the new government, and for protection of the rights of some, but not all, of the people. Notable exceptions at the time were black people and women. Only later were laws passed to protect their rights over the years.

92. B: Marx's focus in *The Communist Manifesto* (1848) and *Das Kapital* (1867) was on the inevitable conflict between the working class and the capitalists who own the means of production. He identified these two opposing forces as the proletariat and the bourgeoisie.

93. A: The federal government has three branches: executive, including the president, the vice president, and the president's cabinet; legislative, including the House of Representatives and the Senate; and judicial, including the Supreme Court and the court system.

94. A: By 1840, more than one third of all Americans lived west of the Alleghenies, but not two thirds. It is correct that in the first half of the 19th century, the American population doubled every 25 years. It is also correct that westward expansion increased as more people moved west during these years. It is correct that there was not a lot of immigration to the US from other countries before 1820. It is also true that foreign immigration to America increased quickly around that time, with most immigrants coming from the British Isles.

95. D: Congress did not have the authority to levy taxes under the Articles of Confederation. Without the ability to levy taxes, there was no way to finance programs, which weakened the government.

96. C: The ancient Mayan civilization was located in Central America. Today, the land of their former empire comprises Guatemala, Belize, Honduras, and El Salvador in Central America and also the Yucatan Peninsula and the south of Mexico. The ancient civilization of the Incas was located in what is now Peru in South America. The ancient civilization of the Aztecs lived in what is Mexico today.

97. C: The 12th Amendment passed in 1804 gave each member of the Electoral College one vote for the president and another for the vice president. Previously, the runner-up in the presidential election became vice president.

98. A: The French and Indian War (Seven Years' War) happened from 1754–1763. The American Revolution happened from 1775–1783. The French Revolution happened from 1789–1799. The War of 1812 happened from 1812–1815.

99. A: The Senate and House of Representatives make up a bicameral legislature. The Great Compromise awarded seats in the Senate equally to each state, while the seats in the House of Representatives were based on population.

100. B: Lines of longitude, which run north-south from pole to pole, are used to separate time zones. Houston, Texas, and Fargo, North Dakota, which are on almost the exact same line of longitude, are both in the Central Time Zone; however, they are not in the same state, do not have the same climate, and are not equidistant from the equator. To calculate distance from the equator, the latitude of the city would need to be known.

101. D: The education of the workforce generally is not treated as a separate, direct input in the basic model of GDP. GDP refers to the value of all goods and services produced by a country in a specific timeframe, and basic models describe that output as depending directly on inputs like labor, capital, and technology. The education of its workforce can impact the quantity of output by increasing worker productivity, but it is usually considered part of labor quality (human capital) rather than a standalone input. GDP is more directly impacted by the size of the workforce, the amount of a country's capital, and the technology already in place. The size of the workforce implies that there are people who are ready and willing to work. The amount of capital means that there is a sufficient number of factories and assets available to create goods and services. Technology refers to the methods, processes, and tools that help labor and capital produce more efficiently.

102. A: Representative government, by which citizens elect officials who share their views and who, in turn, present their views in a democratic system, is not a true democracy in which each individual votes on each issue. As the population of a democracy grows, the practicality of every individual voting on every issue becomes prohibitive to the process.

103. C: The Ottoman Empire joined with the Central Powers in 1914 during World War I. The original Triple Alliance was formed by Austria-Hungary, Germany, and Italy in 1882 and renewed in 1902. The Ottoman Empire signed the Turco-German Alliance in August 1914, joining with the Central Powers. In October 1914, with the bombing of Russian ports on the Black Sea, Turkey formally entered World War I. The Allied Powers of the Triple Entente (Great Britain, France, and Russia) declared war on the Ottoman Empire in November 1914.

104. B: Article I of the Constitution mandates the taking of a census every ten years. The purpose was to be sure that each state was proportionately represented in Congress according to its population as specified in the Constitution. Census data is also used to allocate federal funding for various programs and for shaping economic policies. Individual data collected by the US Bureau of the Census is kept confidential for seventy-two years and does not affect income tax rates. Every state has two seats in the Senate regardless of population.

105. C: The impact of a transaction on third parties not involved in the transaction is known as an externality. An externality can be positive, in which case it's a positive externality or social benefit. An externality can also be negative, in which case it's a negative externality or a social cost.

106. D: Ancient Greek democracy was not completely open to all of the public. However, participating persons were not chosen or excluded based on their respective socioeconomic levels. The city-state of Athens had one of the first and most well-known democracies in ancient Greece. It began around 500 BC. The experiment of Athenian democracy was unique in that it was a direct democracy, meaning people voted directly for or against proposed legislation without any representation such as the House of Representatives and the Senate, as we have in modern democracies.

107. D: The Protestant work ethic is considered by many historians to have contributed to the Industrial Revolution. In Britain, where industrialization started, financial stability encouraged investment in industry, and the eventual dominance of Protestantism is believed to have contributed to a class of entrepreneurs who believed in education, technological progress, and hard work. The other choices are considered effects of industrialization. Mass production enabled the privately owned, for-profit enterprises that characterize capitalist economic systems. Socialism developed as a criticism of capitalism; Karl Marx argued that capitalism polarized societies into owners versus workers. Marx also viewed capitalism as a necessary precursor to socialism within the logical progression of economies. Romanticism also developed in reaction against mechanization and involved using art and literature to contrast nature with the dark side of scientific progress.

108. C: The Underground Railroad was not necessary literally a railroad but a series of clandestine paths to move runaway and freed slaves out of southern states prior to 1865.

109. A: A timeline would be the best way to represent the major events of World War I. Timelines place events in chronological order, with the distance between the events correlated to their interval on the line. A timeline can run in any direction. A thematic map or a flow-line map might also be good at representing this subject, but a political map is restricted to borders and cities; therefore, it would not be able to suggest the changes caused by the war. Bar graphs and pie charts are used to depict quantities and proportions rather than sequences of events.

110. B: Many Americans migrated during World War II, seeking work in war-related factories; boomtowns sprang up as a result. Some Japanese-Americans served in the United States military during World War II; in fact, the all-Japanese 442nd Regimental Combat Team was decorated by the US government for its service. This eliminates choice D. Answer C can be rejected because Caucasian and African-American soldiers served in segregated units. Answer A can be eliminated because consumption actually increased in postwar American society, as production was high and returning US soldiers had income to spend.

111. D: The vice president also serves as the president of the Senate. If a tie occurs in the Senate, the vice president casts his vote to break the tie.

112. A: Of the four answer choices, New York City is the most likely to be considered a modern cultural hearth. A cultural hearth is an area from which cultural trends emanate. Geographers suggest that there were seven original cultural hearths, including Mesoamerica and the Indus River Valley. The modes of living that originated in these areas emanated out into the rest of the world. These days, the cultural hearths tend to be the cities and countries with the most economic power. Of the four answer choices, New York City is clearly the wealthiest and the most influential. The styles and trends that originate in New York City find their way into communities all around the world.

113. D: French chemist Louis Pasteur (1822–1895), considered one of the founders of bacteriology, developed a process of heating and cooling food products like milk and wine that reduces the number of pathogenic microbes to a level that will not cause sickness when ingested. This process is named pasteurization after him. Pasteur also made the first vaccines against both rabies and anthrax. All three of these accomplishments were incredible breakthroughs in preventing fatal diseases. Pasteur's experiments advanced the germ theory of disease, which when first proposed, met strong resistance from those who did not believe microorganisms cause sickness. His work supported its acceptance and colleague Robert Koch's proof of it in 1890. However, Pasteur did not create the first polio vaccine.

114. A: Magnetic poles occur in pairs known as magnetic dipoles. Individual atoms can be considered magnetic dipoles due to the spin and rotation of the electrons in the atoms. When the dipoles are aligned, the material is magnetic. Choices B, C, and D are all magnetic materials. Therefore, the magnetic dipoles in these materials are not randomly aligned. Only choice A has randomly aligned dipoles.

115. D: Once a hypothesis has been verified and accepted, it becomes a theory. A theory is a generally accepted explanation that has been highly developed and tested. A theory can explain data and be expected to predict outcomes of tests. A fact is considered to be an objective and verifiable observation, whereas a scientific theory is a greater body of accepted knowledge, principles, or relationships that might explain a fact. A law is an explanation of events for which the outcome is always the same. A conclusion is more of an opinion and could be based on observation, evidence, fact, laws, or even beliefs.

116. A: Heat on Earth is generated by the sun. The more direct sunlight an area on Earth receives from the sun, the warmer it will be. The earth is most tilted toward or away from the sun at the solstices between spring and summer or between fall and winter. When the Northern hemisphere is tilted away from the sun, all of the countries in the Northern hemisphere experience fall and winter. At that same time, the Southern hemisphere experiences spring and summer. The same is true when the Southern hemisphere experiences fall and winter; the Northern hemisphere experiences spring and summer.

117. C: A population that reaches maximum size and ceases to grow due to a limited availability of resources is said to be at carrying capacity. The carrying capacity of a species is influenced by many factors such as the amount of land or water available, food supply, and predators. Unstable and moving towards extinction are not correct as carrying capacity does not necessarily mean it is unstable or becoming extinct. Shrinking exponentially is also incorrect as the question says it has stopped growing, not that it is reducing in size.

118. A: The center of an atom is known as the nucleus. It is composed of protons and neutrons. The nucleus is positively charged due to protons having a positive charge and neutrons being electrically neutral.

119. C: One way to measure the density of an irregularly shaped object is to submerge it in water and measure the displacement. This is done by taking the mass (40 grams), then finding the volume by measuring how much water it displaces. Fill a graduated cylinder with water and record the amount. Put the object in the water and record the water level. Subtract the difference in water levels to get the amount of water displaced, which is also the volume of the object. In this case, 4.5 liters minus 2.5 liters equals 2 liters. Divide mass by volume (40 grams divided by 2 liters) to get 20 g/L (grams per liter).

120. A: Most organic molecules are not highly soluble in water. A low melting point, covalent bonds, and high flammability are all characteristics of organic molecules. Organic molecules are those that contain carbon atoms, with a few exceptions. Organic molecules tend to be less soluble in water than inorganic salts. They are good at forming unique structures and there are many organic compounds. Examples of organic compounds include hydrocarbons, carbohydrates, lipids, and proteins.

121. D: The formation of sedimentary rock does not include heat. Of the three types of rock—igneous, sedimentary, and metamorphic—heat is essential to two: igneous and metamorphic. Sedimentary rocks are formed by sediments that get deposited and then compacted or cemented together. Sedimentary rocks are classified into detrital, organic, or chemical sediments. Answer A, layering, is correct since sediments can be deposited or otherwise formed in layers. Answer B, cementation, is also called lithification. Answer C, compaction, refers to the pressure forming sedimentary rock leading to cementation.

122. A: Descriptive studies are usually the first form of study in a new area of scientific inquiry. The other answer options here are also forms of scientific study, but they are typically not employed until after initial descriptive studies have been done.

123. A: Heat capacity refers to the amount of heat or thermal energy required to raise the temperature of a specific substance by a given unit. A substance with a higher heat capacity requires more heat to raise its temperature than a substance with a lower heat capacity. The comparison here is that the specific heat capacity of ice is half as much as that of liquid water, so it takes half the amount of energy to increase the same amount of ice one temperature unit than it would if it were liquid water.

124. A: A liquid crystal is best described as having a molecular arrangement is random in some directions and regular in others. A liquid crystal may seem like a contradiction as it seems to refer to two different states of matter. Liquid crystals have properties of both liquids and solids. The molecules of a liquid crystal are loosely bound, allowing them to flow like a liquid, yet they arrange themselves in a repeating pattern like the molecules of a solid which are rigidly fixed in a pattern. Liquid crystals can also organize into layers, but with randomness in the layers.

125. A: The process of absolute dating compares the amount of radioactive material in a rock to the amount that has decayed into another element. Choice B is not usually done. Usually, the stratigraphic layer of rock is used to date the fossils. This is referred to as relative dating. Choice C is incorrect as this would not lead to a correct date since the daughter elements may have a different half-life than the parent material.

126. A: The scientific method is a series of steps to solve a problem. All of the other choices are steps of the scientific method. The steps of the scientific method in order are to make an observation, ask a scientific question, formulate a hypothesis, make a prediction, and test the hypothesis. After the test or experiment is complete, the question should be addressed with the results and used to ask new questions.

127. A: Enzymes are large protein molecules that act as biological catalysts and play an important role in all bodily processes. They are not fat soluble, are not acids, and are not lipids.

128. B: A reaction that uses electricity to drive it. An electrolysis reaction is a chemical reaction that uses electricity to drive it. Electrolysis reactions take place in an electrolytic cell, where one substance will be oxidized and another will be reduced using electrical energy from a battery or other source. Usually, an electrolytic cell is made up of a battery connected to two metal electrodes which are placed in two separate ionic solutions. A salt bridge connects the two beakers of solution and allows positive or negative ions to flow into the solutions as needed to keep the charge balanced as the reaction takes place. The electrode where oxidation takes place is called the anode, which would be connected to the negative terminal on a battery. The electrode where reduction takes place is called the cathode and is connected to the positive terminal of a battery. These reactions are very important for electroplating metals.

129. D: Ocean currents are not controlled by the phase of the moon. The phases of the moon refer to our viewpoint from Earth of the sun's illumination of the moon. Half the moon is illuminated by the sun at any given time. For example, a new moon is one we do not see because the side being lit by the sun is not facing us. The revolution of the moon around the earth affects the ocean tides, providing two highs and two lows at any given point during the day. Wind affects the surface currents of the ocean, while Earth's rotation affects deep currents. Landmasses affect ocean currents as well.

130. C: The majority of the solar energy that reaches Earth is absorbed by the oceans, which make up 71 percent of the Earth's surface. Because of water's high specific heat capacity, oceans can absorb and store large quantities of heat, thus preventing drastic increases in the overall atmospheric temperature.

131. B: Electrons with greater amounts of energy are found farther from the nucleus than electrons with less energy. The principal quantum number describes the level or shell that an electron is in. The lower the number, the closer the electron is to the nucleus and the lower it is in energy.

132. C: In humans, diploid cells are those that contain 46 chromosomes. There are 23 pairs of chromosomes each made up of one chromosome from the father and one from the mother. In meiosis I, each chromosome replicates itself and lines up, or synapses, with its homologous chromosome, and each of the daughter cells ends up with one copy of each of the chromosomes. The two daughter cells at the end of meiosis I are haploid because they contain half of the chromosomes of the parent cell. In humans, this would be 23 chromosomes. However, each of these chromosomes are made of two sister chromatids. In meiosis II, the sister chromatids in the daughter cells separate and result in the production of the gametes. These are also haploid cells because they contain one copy of half of the genetic material of the parent cell. Four haploid cells result from meiosis. Choice A, mitosis, can be eliminated as it refers to the process of cell division where each daughter cell contains exactly the same genetic material as the parent cell. Choice B, telophase, refers to phases of both mitosis and meiosis, during which chromosomes move toward the opposite ends of the cell.

133. B: When land cools off rapidly at night and the ocean water stays relatively warm, it creates a land breeze. Sea breeze, or onshore breeze, occurs when the land heats the air above it. This heated, warmer air is less dense and rises. The cooler air from above the sea and higher sea level pressure creates a wind flow in the direction of the land. Coastal areas often have these cooler breezes. A monsoon is a seasonal wind in southern Asia that blows southwest in one season and northeast in another. The southwest winds in the summer bring heavy rain. The trade winds are the steady easterlies about the equator.

134. A: The structure of the Milky Way galaxy is spiral, meaning it has curved "arms" stretching out from a central point. While spiral galaxies have a flat, disc-like appearance, elliptical galaxies are more three-dimensional and appear to be roughly the same shape regardless of the viewing angle.

135. C: The ball will move forward with respect to the boat. Newton's first law of motion states that an object in motion tends to stay in motion until a force acts to change it. The ball is initially at rest with respect to the boat, but the boat is moving forward. When the front of the boat hits the dock, the boat quickly decelerates, but the ball does not. It continues to move forward because the force acting to stop the boat does not significantly affect the ball. With the ball now moving forward faster than the boat, the ball's motion relative to the boat is forward motion.

136. B: Organisms that belong to the same taxonomic group of family are most alike. In biological taxonomy, the ranks in descending order are Domain, Kingdom, Phylum, Class, Order, Family, Genus, and Species. The ranks become more exclusive and specific as the classification descends. Phylum, class, and order are all higher than the family group. The higher the rank, the fewer requirements it takes to be a member. Two mnemonics for taxonomy are Dashing Kings Play Cards On Fat Green Stools or Dear King Philip Cuts Open Five Green Snakes.

137. B: Recycling and using alternative sources of energy reduce the amount of pollutants introduced into the ecosystem, reduce the potential for disease-related human maladies, and reduce the reliance on nonrenewable resources. Greater production of goods and consumer spending in the future would probably be good for the economy, but not necessarily the environment. Fossil fuels are considered to be a nonrenewable energy resource.

138. C: Venus is not a gas giant. The four gas giants are Jupiter, Saturn, Uranus, and Neptune. While these gas giants are larger than Earth and are composed mostly of gases, Venus is a terrestrial planet that is comparable in size to the Earth.

139. B: If the chemicals heat up, their temperatures increase, and their kinetic energies therefore increase, so energy could not have been obtained from kinetic energy. Chemical reactions also do not typically involve absorption of heat from the environment. Instead, chemical bonds contain some amount of potential energy, which may be released in certain chemical reactions.

140. D: Respiration produces carbon dioxide and water. The net equation of respiration is the reverse of the equation for photosynthesis. Respiration is a series of reactions that consume glucose and oxygen to release energy and produce carbon dioxide and water. Oxygen and glucose are the substances that are broken down in respiration.

141. B: Light travels in straight lines. As light moves from one substance to another, the light rays bend according to the refractive index of each substance. As the light travels through the air, it hits the non-submerged portion of the pencil. The light is reflected from the pencil and this is what we see. However, as the light travels *into* the water, the light waves are bent (refracted), and that light is subsequently reflected and travels to our eyes. What we perceive is a pencil that is no longer whole and straight, but broken and bent. It is refraction that causes this perception.

Although the other distractors are also properties of waves, they are not the reasons why the observer perceives the pencil as bent.

142. C: In 3/4 time, the quarter note is selected as the one beat unit, while in 6/8 time the eighth note is used. Essentially, 6/8 time is the same as the six-note form of 3/4. The only difference is that the eighth note is used as the one-beat unit. Choice (B) is incorrect, as 6/8 time contains 6 beats per measure.

143. A: The most appropriate activity for students at this grade level would be making pinch pots and coil pots. Pinch pots are formed by creating a depression in the center of a ball of clay and smoothing the sides. Coil pots are formed by creating a long, thin length of clay and coiling it to form a pot. Unlike making and attaching handles to pots or throwing pots using a pottery wheel, creating this type of object with clay is appropriate given the fine motor skills and technical sophistication of second graders. The art teacher could model glazing pots using a kiln, but this activity would be too dangerous for young students to attempt on their own.

144. B: The fiber art technique that involves condensing, or matting, fibers together is called felting. Flocking involves applying small fibers to the surface of a fabric to enhance its texture. Macramé fabric is produced by knotting yarns or threads. Plaiting (also known as braiding) involves intertwining multiple threads in a consistent pattern.

145. D: Of the available choices, the activity that most directly supports the learning objective is choice D, asking students to write an essay comparing and contrasting the influence that two famous American artists or artworks had on US society. Choices A and B may be better for promoting general appreciation of artworks, but they do not tie in directly with the part of the objective that talks about the value and role of art in US society. Choice B does not relate well because a timeline does not, on its own, lend itself to either art appreciation or the value and role of art. A timeline would need to be paired with other activities to draw out appreciation or understanding of social value.

146. B: 2:1. Both notes are G, separated by one octave. An octave is the interval between two notes, where the higher note's frequency is exactly twice that of the lower. Choice (A), 1:1, is incorrect, because obviously the notes are not the same. One is higher than the other and therefore has a higher frequency. Choices (C) and (D) are both incorrect, since a frequency ratio of 4:1 or 8:1 refers to differences of two and three octaves, respectively.

147. D: A photograph of a small child standing alone in an empty room would have lots of negative space. Positive space in a painting or photograph is the space occupied by the subject (in this case, the child); negative space is the "empty" part of the composition. The description given of this photograph does not indicate whether the composition is symmetrical or asymmetrical, nor does it indicate whether or not the photograph achieves artistic unity.

148. D: Two observers' differing levels of artistic knowledge, different vantage points, and different cultural beliefs and values could all plausibly explain their differing evaluations of the same painting. An audience's perception of artwork depends on many factors, both physical and psychological. Physical factors include the audience's vantage point (close, far, left, right, above, or below the work of art). Psychological factors include audience members' level of prior knowledge of art and any cultural beliefs or values that might influence their expectations of art.

149. B: In fact, the majority of artists hold postsecondary degrees or certificates. More than half of artists are self-employed, and competition is keen for salaried jobs in the art industry. Annual earnings for artists vary widely, according to the Bureau of Labor Statistics.

150. B: When students engage in extracurricular activities, if they begin to feel overextended, they should not expect (A) or consider this normal; it is a sign that they should quit at least one activity (B). Students should consider not only the abilities and skills they already have (C) and familiar interests but also trying new things in which they are interested as well as the time they have available (D) before they choose extracurricular activities.